LOST AND GONE AWAY

A book is a series of decisions. Sometimes you do not realise you are making them.

Lynn Jenner began writing at the age of 49. Her first book, Dear Sweet Harry – 'the autobiography of an obsession' – won the NZSA Jessie Mackay Award for Best First Book of Poetry in 2011. Jenner's work has been widely published in literary journals, in New Zealand and overseas, including Carcanet's Oxford Poets 2013: An Anthology. She was awarded a PhD in 2013 for the thesis upon which this book is based.

LOST AND GONE AWAY

LYNN JENNER

AUCKLAND
UNIVERSITY
PRESS

First published 2015

Auckland University Press
University of Auckland
Private Bag 92019
Auckland 1142
New Zealand
www.press.auckland.ac.nz

ISBN 978 1 86940 840 4

Publication is kindly assisted by

creative nz
Arts Council of New Zealand Toi Aotearoa

A catalogue record for this book is available from
the National Library of New Zealand

Cover design: Kalee Jackson

Printed in China by 1010 Printing International Ltd

Contents

ONE

The ring story

When everything is turned around

Christchurch, 29 April 2011

Of course, there are rumours that there has been much more looting in the Red Zone than is being officially admitted, the lawyer in Christchurch said when I phoned him about my mother's diamond ring, worth as much as a new European car, and last seen in a jeweller's shop in Cashel Mall five days before the earthquake.

Then there was a silence.

There are rumours that it is the soldiers, he said.

Another silence.

There's such a lot of property in there at the moment and no one really knows who owns it, he said. Most people have turned out to be very honest, he said. But some haven't.

Realistically, I said, what do you think the chances are that my mother will get her ring back?

Nil, he said. You should make an insurance claim.

Sooo, I said, feeling free to speculate now that we had received our advice, what's to stop the jeweller from keeping the ring, not telling his insurance company he has it, and selling the stone in Amsterdam?

Nothing, the lawyer said. I think you should make a claim.

He didn't respond at all to my next suggestion that we could perhaps retain a member of a motorcycle gang to shake down the jeweller on our behalf.

After a long silence he said, let me know if you have any trouble with the insurance company.

*

Sometime in the 1980s my mother had inherited this ring.

A canny Scottish farming woman, doing very well, thank you, was the first owner of the ring. She was a big woman with strong hands. *She* wore the ring to church on Christmas Day and when she went to the races.

She kept the ring wrapped in cotton wool, in a round ivory box with a carved lid inside her wooden jewellery box on her dressing table which had been brought out from Scotland. Huge dark and shiny furniture. Carved edges. Solid brass handles. When she died, at the end of a good long life, she left the ring, along with her maiden name, to her daughter, who, when she died, left the ring to my mother. The huge dark furniture and the Highland flower name went somewhere else.

Himself, as the farming woman called her husband, had inherited one farm, and then he had four, and although he grumbled about the wharfies and their revolutionary tendencies and the effect of wage increases on the cost of shipping, over the years he made pretty fair prices on his mutton and wool. In his fifties he became ill with a disease that caused unbearable pain. A long sea voyage was prescribed. That and morphine. Knowing he would never work again, he gave the farms to his sons, who lost them almost immediately.

My mother wasn't the sort of woman to go to church on Christmas Day or to the races, but for the sake of a farmer's wife from Palmerston and a Highland flower name, which had by then been lost in a sea of men's names, she would sometimes wear the ring. Mostly the ring lived in the ivory box with the carved lid, inside her plain modern jewellery box on her plain modern dressing table, its value something of a worry.

With my father lying beside her in bed, big and warm like a bear, she didn't worry too much. But after he died she took the ring into town and, with a certain amount of formality, placed it in a safe deposit box at the Westpac Bank and there it stayed, in a cool dark box, for a decade or so. Late in 2010 my mother received a letter from her insurance company, saying that the valuation on her ring was out of date. The value of precious stones and gold had been rising rapidly, the letter said, and she should have the ring revalued. What a waste of money having insurance, we said. Surely items in a safe deposit box in the vault of a bank could never be stolen. We thought this was quite funny. We did not consider that the building itself might become a pile of rubble.

My mother decided she should follow the advice of the insurance company and get the ring revalued, but there was a problem. Over the years she had lost the key to the safe deposit box. Some months went by, during which we turned out every corner of her drawers and looked for the key to the safe deposit box, but we never found it. We did find a number of keys for which we could find no locks, but that was no help.

17 February 2011

My mother paid a locksmith to come to the bank, had a new key made for the safe deposit box, opened it, took out the ring in its ivory box and put the box in her purse. Then she walked down a couple of streets to the jeweller in Cashel Mall. I'm not sure why she took the ring to this particular jeweller.

22 February 2011: Earthquake Day

Our main concern was her, but her main concern was her house, her cat, and the fact that there was no power, water or sewerage. I don't know when she first remembered the ring – it might have been after a few days. It is also possible that she remembered straight away and spoke about it, but for a few days I wasn't listening.

I do remember that we talked about it a few times during March. She would use a pragmatic tone. Oh yes, she would say, the ring is almost certainly gone, but it doesn't matter really. People have had such terrible things happen to them. Then we would discuss those terrible things.

As time went by our discussions changed a little. We would each say that the ring was lost. I would say it was lost in the same way as I might refer to the scent of honeysuckle in an English country garden before World War I. She would say the ring was *probably* lost. It took me a few weeks to notice this difference, more time to realise that the person who should do something was me, and more time again to actually do anything.

In the meantime I attended a poetry reading at which a woman collapsed, took out a new mortgage and read books about sculptural representations of the Holocaust.

19 March 2011

I phoned the jeweller's shop in Cashel Mall. There was no reply. I pictured the phone ringing in the Red Zone. Perhaps there were other phones ringing? There was an email address in the jeweller's advertisement in the Yellow Pages, so I sent an email.

> Hello
>
> I don't know how things are with your people and your business – I hope you are all alive and unhurt, and that you might be reading emails. My mother had a diamond ring in being valued on Feb 22. She has asked me to enquire about the ring. We assume it would be in your safe and that you can't access it. Could you please help us with any information on the ring? It isn't as important as people, but it is of sentimental as well as financial value to my mother who is in her eighties. It would be great to hear from you
>
> Lynn

My email came back to me with a message saying the jeweller's inbox was full.

31 March 2011

My mother read an article in the *Listener* about frustrated businessmen who were unable to get in to their businesses in the Red Zone because Civil Defence authorities wouldn't give permission. Gerald (his real name), a jewellery valuer, also from Cashel Mall, was quoted. He found it hard to understand some business people taking a passive attitude, moaning about not being able to get in to their businesses, and meanwhile he had been in to his business three times, he said. My mother thought Gerald might know something about the ring situation because his shop was near the jeweller. I thought that idea was a bit far-fetched, but said I'd try to contact him.

I looked up Gerald's name in the Yellow Pages, phoned his business and the call was redirected to his cellphone which he *answered*. He told me he had been in to his business, got all his stock and computers, and had now moved his business into a new location in Papanui Road. I asked Gerald if he knew how I could contact the jeweller with my mother's ring. He didn't, but he thought perhaps *he* remembered valuing the sparkly old thing. He told me he would check his records in case he still had the ring.

He phoned back the next day and told me he had valued the ring on the morning of 22 February and returned it to the jeweller at lunchtime. He also told me the jeweller's name was Ted (Gerald didn't know his surname) and he gave me Ted's home phone number.

Now there was a trail. My mother took the ring to the jeweller named Ted on 17 February. Ted sent one of his shop assistants, with the ring, to Gerald, the valuer across the road, on 18 February. Gerald took photographs of the ring and wrote up the new valuation on the morning of 22 February then he took the ring across the street, back to Ted the jeweller.

Then nothing.

2 April 2011

After phoning several times, I reached Ted's wife. I asked her to ask him to phone me. He didn't so I phoned him. I caught him at home on the third try. I asked him if any of his staff had been killed or hurt in the quake. He said there were a few cuts and grazes, but nothing more serious. He had a broad Devon accent and a defeated air. I distrusted him instantly.

I explained the trail to him and asked him if he had any ideas about what might have happened to the ring.

Was it in his safe? I asked, thinking of a business like the Mercedes factory where every step would be guided by a protocol that never varied. He told me that he was only the owner and did not actually work there, so he did not know how the ring would have been handled, and he had no idea where the ring would have been at the time of the earthquake. He had not been allowed in to his business since the earthquake, he said. He also said that he might not be continuing in business. I felt as though I was trying to hold on to a small undomesticated animal. It was wriggling and its eyes were darting from side to side, looking for a dark hole it could run away into.

He said he would ask his staff if they remembered the ring and get back to me.

He didn't.

9 April 2011

I phoned Ted again. He repeated that he had not been in to his business and did not know anything about the property which was there at the time of the earthquake. He made no offer to keep in touch, so I said I would phone him weekly to see how things were progressing. I wanted to keep his mind on our problem.

17 April 2011

I rang Ted again. He prevaricated some more. His shop was in Zone 12, he said, as if that was important. The closest he had been to his shop was the fence. Etc. Etc. At one stage he began a vivid description of the minutes straight after the quake.

He and all the staff scrabbling around in the broken glass and bricks, picking up whatever jewellery they could lay their hands on, taking it down to the basement where they had a wall safe. Power off, the basement in total darkness, after-shocks and sirens and people screaming.

These were the first things he said which I believed.

They shoved, that was his word, *shoved*, whatever they had in their hands into the safe, but they were only able to lock one of its two locks. After that, he said, the police came and made them leave the building.

I was at a loss to know how to do any more for my mother, who, I now realised, felt guilty that, after three generations, the ring had been lost *on her watch*. Those were her words. My partner and I talked about options. Could you phone the police if you suspected someone of an *intention* to commit a crime? We thought not. What if Ted was not dishonest – just useless? Looking at this now, I see that a couple of weeks went by in this phase. I can think of no reason why so much time passed, when the next step is so obvious.

28 April 2011

I emailed my mother's solicitor for advice. I thought about asking a lawyer near home but decided that a lawyer who was doing business in Christchurch would have more of a feel for what was going on than a lawyer from Paraparaumu. I was imagining Ted in court as I wrote this, so I was careful.

> Good morning Kerry
>
> I have made a time to talk with you tomorrow, April 29 at 2.30 about the best way for us to proceed regarding a diamond ring that belongs to my mother and is missing in the earthquake. The ring was at X Jewellers being valued on Feb 22. There is

no dispute about that. The ring is an antique, with sentimental value as well as an insured value of more than $50,000.

My mother has asked me to help her to recover the ring, if at all possible. At this stage, I am uneasy about the attitude of Ted X, the business owner, having found him evasive at best and probably lying once that I am aware of.

I wonder if Ted is making any reasonable effort to locate the rings and what the standard operating procedure would have been for handling rings like this – would they always be put into a safe on return from valuation? And therefore what the chances are of recovering them from the safe?

And I wonder what is to stop a business owner in this situation from claiming from his insurance, leaving my mother to claim from her insurance, and recovering the ring himself?

I imagine the building will soon be demoslished [*sic*]. Once that happens there is no further chamce [*sic*] to reciver [*sic*] the rings, so there is possibly some urgency.

I have tried to engage Ted in discussion about the recovery of the rings but he is not helpful. I have also left a message for the other owner, Mr B, (17/04/11) asking him to contact me and have not had a response.

I would like advice about what to do next. I imagine there are lots of situations a bit like this in Christchurch.

Lynn

1 May 2011

Two days after I spoke with the lawyer, Ted phones. He has been allowed in to his business for fifteen minutes, during which time he has retrieved my mother's ring, which he is now keen to hand over to us. I ask him to keep it until I am next down in Christchurch, on 23 May. He agrees. I am to phone him when I arrive in Christchurch.

23 May 2011

I arrive in Christchurch. The shuttle driver tells me there is a vagrant living in the Grand Chancellor Hotel, eating the food and drinking the drinks left behind in twenty-six storeys of minibars. He follows the sun around the building to keep warm and sleeps in a different room each night, according to the driver.

The hotel building, supported with truckloads of concrete while complex negotiations are going on about who would pay for demolition, is on a clear lean. I see that as we pass nearby. Many of its windows are broken, curtains flap in the wind, and there are stories in the paper of expensive belongings people had left behind in the panic of evacuating the building.

According to the driver, the man was spotted by police as a mobile dark shape on infra-red thermal imaging equipment, the building itself having reached the ambient temperature of Christchurch in May.

After that there are earnest conversations between the passengers about how the man could have got past the cordon and whether he had been homeless before the earthquake or not, the answer to this last question apparently making a huge difference to the whole situation.

24 May 2011

I phone Ted to arrange the handover. He suggests I meet him at 7 pm the next evening, in the car park of a disused garden centre in Marshlands Road. I say no to the garden centre car park in the dark. I suggest we meet at a BP petrol station near the garden centre which I assume will be better lit and have more people around. He agrees. Don't forget, he says, there is a charge of $175 for the valuation. Bring a cheque made out to X Jewellers.

25 May 2011

11 am
I ask my mother if she would rather stay home while I go get the ring, but she says no, she wouldn't dream of letting me go by myself.

2 pm
We drive out to the BP station, work out the direction Ted will come from and where we can park and watch who is coming and going.

5 pm
We put two torches in the car, one with a big heavy handle. We tell two other people where we are going and instruct them to call the police if we are not home by 9 pm. Down the phone from Raumati, my partner hums the Harry Lime theme.

6.45 pm
We arrive at the BP station fifteen minutes early. I park and we begin surveillance. After a while we see one car with a woman driver pull up. I write down its number plate. Then another car, and another, each with a woman driver. I write down all the number plates because when someone finds our car and our battered bodies, the number plates will help them find who did it. Then, about 7.07 pm, Ted pulls up in an old grey Toyota Corolla. I know it's him because I had asked him what sort of car he drove. We stay in the shadows, watching what is happening. A little pattern emerges. A woman gets out of her car and approaches Ted's car. He gets out and they walk to the rear of his car. In the red light of his tail light, he gets a package out of the boot, unwraps it, shows the woman something, she signs a piece of paper and goes back to her car. She drives off. After the third woman has driven off, I drive our car up behind Ted's car and leave the lights on. We wait.

He comes over to the driver's window. Lynn? he says.
I introduce my mother and myself. Is it OK if I get in the car, he asks. Yes, I say, and he gets into the back seat. I turn the inside car light on. He could easily hit me on the head from behind, and I should have thought of that but now it is too late.

He gets out an envelope. This is the valuation, he says. He hands us photographs of the ring. We hand him the cheque. I get out the big torch and shine it on the photographs. He gets a package out of his pocket, unwraps it and holds the ivory ring box out to my mother. We open the box and compare the ring with the photograph. I ask my mother if she is satisfied that this is her ring. She says yes.

Ted hands her a piece of notepad paper with 'I acknowledge receipt of my ring' written in ballpoint pen. Sign here please, he says. My mother signs.

Ted sighs and folds over somehow. When he starts talking it's all about insurance. You take out insurance and you think you've got yourself covered for everything, he says, and then when something like this happens, you realise that there is so much that you never even thought about. It's all just business, he says. If they have four billion in claims and they can hold onto that money for an extra couple of weeks even, the interest on that is probably the size of my whole claim.

The insurance company is keeping him waiting, he says. He phones them every week and each time he talks to a different person. They won't say whether they will be paying him out. He thinks they are too scared to tell him the decision. He wants them to pay him out for a total loss, he says, but they want to set him up in new premises because that is cheaper for them. If they investigate you, and they find that you needed money *before* the earthquake, they won't pay out, he says. I wonder if the jewellery shop in Cashel Mall was in trouble. I am trying to think of a way to ask that, but by then my mother has had enough of the ancient mariner's story, and she dismisses him rather firmly.

We drive home across the city in the dark. There aren't many of us on the road. To my right, as we drive down Fitzgerald Avenue, I see the Red Zone. Actually I do not see anything. The centre of the city is as dark as the inside of a cow.

Postscript: December 2014

Sometimes I wonder if all this really happened, but, except for the story of the vagrant, it did. I think I made that up. When I wrote the ring story, the week after we retrieved the ring, it had a happy ending. I suppose I assumed there would be many other happy endings in Christchurch. Nearly four years later, there are still families living in sheds, and thousands of others living in their broken houses while they battle their way through the insurance system. Kerry, the kind lawyer who advised us so calmly, has died. All of this makes the return of the ring a nice moment in a big complicated story.

*

TWO

The panorama machine

Quotes are justified (to show their canonical quality) and my contributions are unjustified. No pun intended.

A boy called Josef is led to the panorama by his grandmother who loves this outing as much as he does. She pays for them to enter. They climb up on stools and place their eyes to a set of eye holes, a little like binoculars. Each time they visit they see a sequence of pictures. *A Native Wedding in Samoa*, or *Eskimo Fur Traders*. One day it was *The Emperor's Birthday*. The grandmother enjoyed this one particularly, humming the Radetzky March all the way home in the tram and conducting an invisible orchestra with tiny movements of her lilac-gloved right hand.

*

It doesn't matter that you must sit a little awkwardly to reach from the stool to the metal eyepiece and that you must sit rigid in this posture if you want to see the images. It doesn't matter that your breath condenses on the metal of the eyepiece, drips onto your face and runs down your cheeks like tears unless you lick each drop as it passes your mouth, which the grandmother says is unhygienic.

*

Josef thinks it a little sad that all the people and distant other lands remain inside the panorama machine, no matter how many times he looks at them.

As a child, I had a book called *From Ur to Rome*. White sand fell from the binding. Black birds stood on one yellow leg; the other leg bent and stretched in mid-stride. Each bird had one round orange eye. Swallows arrived in spring, so many that they darkened the sky, sweet water flowed underground and the black centre of each of the painted eyes of the dead queen was a forbidden cave.

> *From Ur to Rome*, by K. M. Gadd. London: Ginn and Co., 1937.
>
> 'This textbook tells the story in language suited to eleven year olds, describing the everyday life of the people in the ancient world rather than their political history. A surprising amount of detail is given in so short a sketch, and the book is well illustrated . . . It is designed to serve as a quarry in which the pupils can search for answers to their own questions . . .'

Lying on my stomach on the floor wherever a square of sun fell down, I read and re-read this book. After a while something different would happen. Sometimes we moved to a different house. Sometimes a new book would arrive, and I would switch my allegiance. Sometimes I would wear out a book, and my parents would take me into town on the bus on a Friday night, to see if they could buy another copy for me.

In this way they taught me, although, in the style of those times, nothing was said, that each time you read a book, you read it differently.

1938: the year the first New Zealand Labour government passed the Social Security Act and the year of the Anschluss.

The Classical Association's unnamed reviewer appreciated the emphasis Kathleen M. Gadd placed on the *everyday life* of people in the ancient world, this life understood and explained through the production of drawings and photographs of objects from that time.

Everyday life: Objects of human rather than artistic interest . . .

1. A spinning top, terra cotta, eighth century BCE
2. Doll with castanets, terra cotta, circa 350 BCE
3. Baby feeder, pottery, fourth century BCE, with inscription, 'drink don't drop'
4. Miniature wine jug, 425–400 BCE
5. Rattle in the form of a pig, terra cotta, third–second centuries BCE
6. Two figurines: a woman grinding grain and another baking bread.

Grouped in this case by the British Museum in 2001, under categories such as 'sacrifice', 'gods', 'reading and writing', 'women', 'trade and transport'.

No category for 'slaves', 'foreigners' or 'torture'.[1]

1 Page Du Bois, *Slaves and Other Objects*, Chicago: The University of Chicago Press, 2003, pp. 39–42.

In 2008 I made a list of all the books I have worn in and worn out to see if they had anything in common. How lifeless my fetish objects looked in this list, but how each had shimmered and glowed in its day.

The list of worn-out books exists. That is a fact. This list is a guide to my life and at the same time a record of it, following every turn and twist as closely as my bank statements. The journey marked out by all those books is strange, unintentionally amusing and informative in its own way but, in another way, as puzzling as if there had been no record made.

At the age of nine I went on record, saying to George Ashton, the principal of my primary school, that I wanted to 'be' an archaeologist. He went on record too, saying that I could 'be' anything I wanted. (These were, in an austere way, generous times.) Looking back, I see that archaeology has always been my intent, although my activities went under different names at different times.

Mostly I find books and facts in my excavations. Books are my listening and viewing devices, my undersea cables, my hearing aids, my best friends in troubled times and my weapon of choice. I am not easily cowed by their origins or their methods, even when these are august. I look them straight in the eye and take them on if I think they are wrong and I mess about with them quite a bit.

Facts make astounding patterns when placed side by side, and are, in addition, much less self-conscious than anything writers imagine. Facts reek of human purposes.

Sometimes, rising up from a pile of facts or a book, and hovering over it, is something I think of as a moment of knowledge. I could use a word like 'nugget' to signify the value of a particular piece of knowledge and hint at the exhausting labour of finding it. But since I do not perceive knowledge as having edges or substance you can test with your teeth, a word like 'nugget' would be misleading. A shape in ectoplasm would be closer. My knowledge lacks authority, I'm afraid.

Freud had a collection of small objects from antiquity, some no larger than a chess piece, some a few inches tall, arranged in a line on his desk in Vienna. He would have seen these vases and human figures whenever he raised his eyes from his writing. Also on his desk: a clock, a lamp, a knife to open letters and some other objects whose purpose I do not know. I imagine they are, in some way, tools of writing, but they could also be medical implements he used in his work with patients or on himself.

In June 1938, Freud left Vienna, accompanied by his wife Martha, his daughter Anna, two maidservants, his chow and his doctor. They were met in England by other members of the family who had come to England earlier. At first the family lived in temporary accommodation. But in their house in South Hampstead Freud's son Ernst reconstructed the old man's Vienna office. Freud's desk, where all his precious objects stood in a line in front of the blotter, was just as it had been, even if its context was very different. As a middle-aged woman, I interpret Ernst's reconstruction of his father's desk as a small gesture of consolation for the loss of the room, the house and the life in Vienna. The equivalent of touching his arm. But perhaps filial piety might be more accurate.

Freud described analysis as a form of archaeology. I felt a small movement inside my body when I read this, as if the tongue of a lock had emerged from its cavity, extended itself towards a new place, found that it fitted and settled there.

Freud had several high-ranked international supporters who lobbied for him to be allowed to leave Austria. It may seem today as if there could be no other possible outcome than that Freud, a famous man, would be allowed to die in England from the cancer he had had for many years. But his sister Dolfi died in Theresienstadt and his sisters Mitzi, Rosa and Pauli died in Treblinka, their relationship to a famous man no protection.

In 1938, while they waited for permission to enter England and permission to leave Austria, Freud's son Martin and daughter Anna were briefly arrested. Copies of Freud's *Complete Works* were confiscated and burned. Storm troopers came to Freud's house on 15 March and took away all the household money and contents of the safe. The Gestapo searched the house for political material. The contents of Freud's bank account were confiscated.

From his desk in England in November 1938, Freud wrote an essay called 'A Word about Anti-Semitism'. A copy of this essay, in cursive script, is part of an odd collection of material supplied in a pocket of a biography of Freud that I bought this year. Freud's handwriting is strongly sloped and the words are close together, making it almost impossible to read them. The author must have placed the document there to evoke the mood of 1938, I decided. I do not imagine that I would ever be able to translate Freud's mood at this time, even if I could read the words.

It is hard, from over here, to *really believe* that there was a Vienna where Freud worked and where his books were burned, where scholars who couldn't save themselves pressed suitcases full of unpublished manuscripts into the hands of friends and even strangers. You can hear about it. You may think you believe it. But there is always some part of you that is holding itself back from the ending.

Walter Benjamin's dream:

. . . I saw myself in Goethe's study. It bore no resemblance to the one in Weimar. Above all, it was very small and had only one window. The side of the writing desk abutted on the wall opposite the window. Sitting and writing at it was the poet, in extreme old age. I was standing to one side when he broke off to give me a small vase, an urn from antiquity, as a present. I turned it between my hands. An immense heat filled the room. Goethe rose to his feet and accompanied me to an adjoining chamber, where a table was set for my relatives. It seemed prepared, however, for many more than their number. Doubtless there were places for my ancestors, too. At the end, on the right, I sat down beside Goethe. When the meal was over, he rose with difficulty and by gesturing I sought leave to support him. Touching his elbow, I began to weep with emotion.[2]

---

2 Walter Benjamin, 'No. 113', *One-Way Street and Other Writings*, trans. Edmund Jephcott and Kingsley Shorter, London: Verso, 1979, p. 47.

A letter from Sigmund Freud to a friend:

When, finally, on the afternoon of our arrival, I stood on the Acropolis and cast my eyes around upon the landscape, a surprising thought suddenly entered my mind: 'So all this really *does* exist, just as we learned at school . . .'

It must be that a sense of guilt was attached to the satisfaction in having gone such a long way: there was something about it that was wrong, that from earliest times had been forbidden. It was something to do with a child's criticism of his father . . . . It seems as though the essence of success was to have got further than one's father, and as though to excel one's father was still something forbidden . . .

In our particular case, the very theme of Athens and the Acropolis in itself contained evidence of the son's superiority. Our father had been in business, he had no secondary education, and Athens could not have meant much to him. Thus what interfered with our enjoyment of the journey to Athens was a feeling of 'filial piety'.[3]

---

3 Sigmund Freud, 'A Disturbance of Memory on the Acropolis' (1936), *Standard Edition of the Complete Psychological Works*, second edn, trans. J. Strachey, London: Hogarth Press and The Institute of Psychoanalysis, 1964, vol. 22, pp. 239–248.

Bruno Schulz:

The primeval word was a shimmering aura circling around the sense of the world, was a great universal whole. The word in its common usage today is only a fragment, remnant of some former all-embracing, integral mythology. That is why it possesses a tendency to grow back, to re-generate and complete itself in full meaning. The life of the word consists in tensing and stretching itself toward a thousand connections, like the cut-up snake in the legend whose pieces search for each other in the dark . . . . Poetry happens when short circuits of sense occur between words, a sudden regeneration of the primeval myths.[4]

---

4 Bruno Schulz, 'The Mythologizing of Reality', trans. Mikolaj Dutsch and Josef Hahn, *The Picture Chamber of Bruno Schulz – The Final Work of a Genius – Mobile Installation by Benjamin Geissler*, ed. Benjamin Geissler, Hamburg: Benjamin Geissler, 2012, p. 24.

According to a book I found, there are sub-groups of missing people, each with its own name – Despondents, for example, are quite different from The Overdue, The Stranded and The Criminal. I thought at the beginning that I might call out those names and see who showed up.

Then I would write about the way a search takes hold of some people and never lets them rest.

As I say, this was my initial intention.

About this time a friend suggested that I read Anne Carson's translation of Sappho.[5] For some time after that, her text took centre stage, its one-sided brackets hanging like empty sleeves.

5 Anne Carson, *If Not, Winter: Fragments of Sappho*, trans. Anne Carson, New York: Vintage Books, 2003.

Arthur S. Way:

The fame of Sappho, as the greatest poetess of all time, rests mainly on tradition, which for us moderns is confirmed by one complete poem, two incomplete ones, and over 170 fragments, one consisting of six lines, ten of four, seven of three, twenty-seven of two, and the rest of not more than one line, sometimes of only one word. No other poet inherits such a great fame on so slight a foundation. Yet none is, by universal consent, more incontestably pre-eminent in his sphere.[6]

---

6 Arthur S. Way, Introduction, *Sappho, and the Vigil of Venus*, trans. A. S. Way, London: Macmillan and Co. Limited, 1920.

Guy Davenport:

There is so little Sappho that the reader with even a little Greek can read the substantial fragments in an afternoon. There are many fine translations of Sappho in English (though none, to my knowledge, that includes all but the utterly hopeless fragments without whole words in them anywhere), and the only excuse for making a new one lies in the richness of her poetry: each translator reflects what he sees, performing not so much a linguistic as a critical act, the closest possible rendering of his appreciation. Many of the fragments are mere words and phrases, but they were once a poem, and, like broken statuary, are strangely articulate in their ruin.[7]

---

7 Guy Davenport, Preface, *Sappho, Poems and Fragments*, trans. Guy Davenport, Ann Arbor: The University of Michigan Press, 1965, p. 19.

In 1896, Egypt was occupied by the British although still part of the Ottoman Empire. British interests had owned the Suez Canal since 1875, and Britain had a strong influence on the politics and financial structures of Egypt.

Bernard Grenfell and Arthur Hunt, from Queen's College, Oxford, went to Egypt with funding from the Egypt Exploration Fund, looking for pieces of papyrus.

Grenfell and Hunt settled on a small town 120 miles south of Cairo called Oxyrhynchus, meaning 'sharp nosed [fish]', for their dig. Part of the same site is now a village called el Bahnasa. On the outskirts of town was a group of low mounds. Almost as soon as they began to dig, Grenfell and Hunt realised it was the rubbish dump of a once thriving town dating from the period of Hellenistic Egypt. Grenfell and Hunt supervised hundreds of Egyptian workers excavating the rubbish mounds. For months they piled tiny scraps of torn papyrus into reed baskets, sifted and deciphered them, before packing them up into Huntley & Palmers biscuit tins and sending them back to Oxford.

Grenfell and Hunt's excavations continued into the twentieth century, stopping only for World War I, until Grenfell died in 1926. Hunt then continued the work until he died in 1934. Most of the fragments are records of everyday life: bills and receipts, IOUs, invitations, inventories, tickets, laundry lists. But one page seemed to record some of the sayings of Jesus and another was attributed to Euclid. Grenfell and Hunt found another tiny scrap, dating from the third (or sixth) century CE, in 1897. This was a copy of a poem by Sappho, a new poem previously unknown, and now referred to as Fragment 5: 'To the Nereids'.

In the end there were crates and crates of such fragments, and the process of dealing with them goes on to this day. The Egypt Exploration Society began, slowly, to edit and publish the finds. Despite having reached their sixty-sixth volume in the series, the findings are still being published, and the Ashmolean Museum at Oxford still holds crates of fragments in its basement.

In 2011 the University of Oxford invited ordinary people to help transcribe fragments of papyrus, using an online transcription tool.[8] No prior knowledge of Greek is required, they say, however it has been necessary to provide a chart which shows combinations of letters which are possible and not possible in Greek and also a list of reasons why Greek text may include combinations of letters which are

---

8 'Ancient Lives', *ancientlives.org*, University of Oxford, accessed 10 September 2012.

not possible in Greek. Names imported from Hebrew, for example.

I may be wrong but I guess this invitation to the public means that the words on all the big pieces of papyrus have already been transcribed, forming the basis of many academic careers, and that the volume of tiny fragments, as yet un-transcribed, is a bit of a nuisance. Although held at Oxford University, the papyri remain the property of the Egypt Exploration Society.

Papyrus was a good material. It gave people a way of recording ideas and passing them easily from one person to another. But it took a lot of time and some effort to make this place to put writing. The first step was to find the papyrus plant. *Cyperus papyrus*, the Egyptian papyrus plant, was common in ancient Egypt, growing mostly along the edge of waterways.

To make the writing surface, you strip off the outside layer of the stem, and cut the inside soft part into even-sized strips. Then you pound them. You lay the strips side by side to make the first layer. Then you make a second layer, laying the strips at right angles to the first layer. Finally, you wet the whole thing and put a rock or some other heavy object on top and leave the wet squishy pile of material for about three weeks. The juice of the papyrus plant glues everything together and the rock and the heat of the sun make the squishy plant material thin and solid. At the end of the three weeks there is a surface to write on. One piece of papyrus might be twenty centimetres square.

Since it took many layers of wrapping to encase a mummy, it is thought by archaeologists that the fragment of Sappho's poem known as *L-P 67*, which was found in the late nineteenth century CE wrapped around a mummified crocodile, is an ancient example of recycling.

The fact that the wrappings of the crocodile were found to include fragments of papyrus covered with writing, and that one of these fragments was later included by scholars in the body of poems attributed to Sappho, was thought to mean that at the time of making the mummy, the poem by Sappho was seen as less valuable than the piece of papyrus.

Oh! The crocodile wrapped in words.

Huntley & Palmers are proud of the history of their biscuit tins, especially 'the square 5lb and 10lb . . . tins which could be used as storage for virtually any sort of cargo'.[9] During the Fourth Anglo-Ashanti War in 1896, His Royal Highness Prince Henry of Battenberg, who was married to one of Victoria's daughters, died of malaria on a cruiser off the coast of Sierra Leone. Thanks to a modern version of the traditional naval practice of carrying home the body of someone important submerged in rum, he was able to be buried with proper ceremony only three weeks later in St Mildred's church on the Isle of Wight.

In the case of Horatio Nelson, who died in 1805, the only option had been to fold him into a barrel for his journey home, but by the time Prince Henry died, he was able to be carried home lying down, in a tank made out of Huntley & Palmers biscuit tins. Lying down is much more dignified than being folded in half. The metal tank may also have offered better protection from sailors who were known to tap a barrel and drink the rum even when there was a body inside.

9 'When is a Biscuit Tin Not a Biscuit Tin?', *HuntleyandPalmers.org.uk*, accessed 22 May 2010.

Biscuit tins in the Sudan. On 2 September 1898 the British defeated Mohammed Ahmad, who believed that he was the Messiah, at the battle of Omdurman. This battle was said to be necessary in order to maintain British control over Egypt and the Suez Canal. Some captured Sudanese swords had scabbards with metal bands cut from Huntley & Palmers biscuit tins, with the firm's name clearly visible.

And Bibles in Uganda. Bibles and prayer books for the natives were packed into biscuit tins to protect the books from white ants. 'African Boys, about 1903'[10]

10 *HuntleyandPalmers.org.uk*, accessed 22 May 2010; photograph in the collection of Reading Museum (REDMG:1997.130.620).

Grenfell and Hunt's letter to *The Times*, 14 May 1906:

The evidence of documents found below the literary texts shows that the latter must have been thrown away in the fifth century; but the manuscripts themselves are chiefly of the second or third century . . . . It is doubtful whether continuous sheets of much length can be built up out of the innumerable fragments, which range in size from some lines to a few letters.

This is the more regrettable because the owner of the library was much interested in the Lyric poets. His collection included two or three manuscripts apparently of Sappho.

Mysteries and speculations

1. Sappho lived on the island of Lesbos in the sixth century BCE.
2. 'She' may not have been a single person; perhaps she was a school?
3. Her name was not pronounced 'Saffo'. It would probably have sounded more like 'Ppppsappoppo'. Speculative performances of her name, emphasising movements of lips, are to be found on YouTube.[11]
4. Her poems were composed to be sung to the lyre. Except for what remains in translations of her words, all her music is lost.
5. The lyrics were sung in Aeolic Greek, a vernacular dialect which has now disappeared. No one really knows the context in which these lyrics were sung.
6. There was writing in Greek in the sixth century BCE, but Sappho's poems were not written down until perhaps 300 years after she died.
7. On papyrus, text is written in columns, without word division, punctuation or lineation.
8. Of the nine books of lyrics that Sappho is said to have composed, which might have amounted to about 10,000 words, one poem has survived complete. All the rest are fragments.
9. Oxyrhynchus has now been largely submerged by an irrigation project.

---

11 See artist/poet George Quasha's 'video invocation' of people attempting to say the name 'Sappho'.

Three reconstructions

1. In the early 2000s Michael Gronewald and Robert Daniel, working in the archives of Cologne University, found a document dated to the third century BCE and used as part of a mummy's covering, or cartonnage. This fragment recorded quotations from three of Sappho's poems. Gronewald and Daniel described this discovery in a German papyrology journal in 2004.
2. One of these quotations, when put together with a fragment found in Oxyrhynchus in 1922, made poem 58, a bittersweet reflection on ageing.
3. Martin West published the new poem in the original Greek and in English translation in the *Times Literary Supplement* on 24 June 2005, along with a short reflection about the youth of each year's new undergraduates.

Orpheus, son of Apollo, was the most famous musician the world has ever known. When he played his lyre animals crowded round, lions lay tame at his feet, mountains would move towards the sound and trees would bend and pull up their roots to hear his music.

When he lost his wife, Eurydice, his songs became so sad that they broke the heart of anyone who heard them. He mourned alone on a mountain until one day the sound of Orpheus's lyre was gone and was never heard again. Some said the gods, unable to bear his lamentation, struck him with lightning. In another version of the story, the women of Thrace tore off his head.

In the gentler version, where Orpheus was struck by lightning, his lyre floated down a river and out into the sea, playing all the while. In both versions the lyre washed up on the shores of the island of Lesbos, where it lay neglected, overgrown with vines and buried under leaves.

The winds of the Lesbos are known for their melodies, and nightingales sing more sweetly there than anywhere else. No bird sang more sweetly than Sappho.

After a day of reading Sappho, I am on the beach, compelled to stare into the fire as it sinks below the horizon. The tip of every wave is shiny metal; all of us, strangers, neighbours and lovers, turn to each other and offer blessings; all of us knowing our part in this and no one awkward or reluctant. This moment is so lyrical that I hurry home to find it in the poems.

I do not find this prize –

I find instead, *brightness* that strikes
the eye, I find the universal measurement of time
from her time until there is no time –

I find the gift of light –
But never the sun *dying* for the day

Yahrzeit is the Jewish name for commemorating the death of a parent or close relative at the time of year when the person died.[12] Yahrzeit is marked at home by lighting a candle which burns all day. Some fast on this day, some abstain from eating meat or drinking wine. Some visit the grave of the dead person.

Special candles are available but any candle that will burn for twenty-four hours can be used. Some families, concerned about the safety of an open flame which burns for twenty-four hours, use a special yahrzeit lamp. There are no special prayers or blessings that must be recited when lighting a yahrzeit candle, but often, at this time, people will spend time in introspection or share memories of the dead person.

---

12 In English, the word can also be spelled 'yartzeit', 'yortzeit' or 'jahrzeit'.

The poem about the candle

The purchase of a yartzeit candle in the presence of tradition
and an absence of belief occupies him. The placing
of the candle in a cheap glass cup on the kitchen bench
occupies him. The interest of a third-century scholar
named Athenaios in the possible distinction between
a whore and a courtesan occupies him.

Ignoring the yartzeit candle, chopping vegetables
and pouring *milk* occupy him. The repeated *holding*
of the cheap glass cup tilted towards his face
and the striking of the match occupy him. The time
it will take for the candle to *burn* occupies him. The aura
of the brother; the peculiar way he could fold his *legs*
occupies him. This form, its fire, *the dim dim light*

In one sense the poem about the candle belongs to Glenn Kurtz, who happened to be reading *If Not, Winter*, Anne Carson's translation of Sappho, as the anniversary of his brother's death approached.[13] Glenn Kurtz is the man who bought the yahrzeit candle, wondered if lighting it would have any meaning which was real to him, and worried about how to remember his brother in a way that was in some way true to the man his brother was. Kurtz wrote about these things in an essay in the *Southwest Review* in 2010.[14]

Glenn Kurtz is an established writer. He lives in a country where a living can be earned writing and talking about books. His essay is six pages long. In this space he patiently unfolds and dissects the story of reading the book and the story of living through the month leading up to the lighting of the candle. He examines these experiences in a cool morning light. Then he tilts the two things towards each other and looks at whether that movement changes the way light falls on each. This last action caused me to write two poems.

All the way through the essay I had a strong sense of the man as well as the author. I could feel him taking pieces of the two experiences and rubbing them between his thumb and his first two fingers, as I might feel a piece of fabric to learn its qualities. I could hear his voice as he speaks to himself and to his readers about what he is thinking. I noticed how strict

---

13 I am not sure there is such a thing as chance in reading choices.

14 Glenn Kurtz, 'What Remains: Sappho and Mourning', *Southwest Review*, vol. 95, nos 1 & 2 (2010), reproduced at *poems.com/special_features/prose/essay_kurtz.php*, accessed 8 February 2011.

he was with himself, alert for any backsliding to some cheap and easy version of grief that might infringe the rights of the dead. As he brings his arguments together, he says that he has learned something new about mourning from juxtaposing his own loss of a brother with Anne Carson's translation and its 'aesthetic of loss', but I found that I could not put my finger on what it was that he had learned.

I read his essay several more times, looking for the places in the text where something seems to change. I started marking those places with a pink highlighter pen. After a while I found that I had fallen into a sort of trance where most words passed in a blur but a few words seemed to jump out at me. I stopped marking these jumping words with the pink pen and started writing them down. After four or five phrases I looked at what I had written. I liked the particularity of the man's actions and I liked the spaces it left.

Almost every word in the poem about the candle comes from Kurtz's article. I changed 'cereal' to 'milk', which I thought more comforting. I also translated the American 'kitchen counter' to the New Zealand 'kitchen bench' and paraphrased a comment about religious beliefs. Rather more significantly, I added the idea of deliberate ignoring.

Re-reading his article a year after writing the poem, it is clear that I rewrote his story to make this poem. I am not sure whether I used 'occupies him' in that repeated way because I didn't believe him that the candle sat inert for a week while he lived around it, or because I needed a verb.

The muttering poem

It is the death day and so
the light returns to view the soul
the dead we have lost but
this ritual has little to
do with his soul – if
I believed the flame the persistence
I could rest

The truth is something very different –
I do not hear a presence
yet the image flickers.
This *is* a dim dim light

Scholarship also tricks us –
Nothing fills the silence
in this broken aching form.
The candle flickers – I feel
a different reanimation from
damaged papyrus and open space
all faithful
but not the one who lived.
This explains the gravity the tenderness
This *alone* on an otherwise blank page

The muttering poem had a different genesis. At the same time as I was reading Glenn Kurtz's article, I was also 'reading' Jonathan Safran Foer's *Tree of Codes*, which is an erasure and die-cut of *The Street of Crocodiles* by Bruno Schulz.

Tree of Codes contains words, punctuation marks and the usual white spaces a reader would expect in an erasure. It also contains deep rectangular holes of various sizes. These take the reader down to lower levels of the book in a physical way.

'[*The Street of Crocodiles*] is a book I've always loved,' Safran Foer said in an interview with Heather Wagner from *Vanity Fair*. 'Some things you love passively, some you love actively. In this case, I felt the compulsion to do something with it.'[15]

I am shocked by Safran Foer's physical surgery on a loved book.

I imagine that early on, Safran Foer would have marked with a pencil or a highlighter the sections he wanted to keep, the parts he wanted whited out and the parts he wanted cut out. But, at a certain point, Safran Foer, or his assistants, must have cut into the pages with a knife. And, even worse, he would surely have needed to cut several copies before he found exactly the right sections for the die-cut.

'Whose book is this? Is it your book? Or is it Bruno Schulz's book? You are using his words,' Wagner asks.

---

15 Heather Wagner, 'Jonathan Safran Foer Talks *Tree of Codes* and Conceptual Art', *Vanityfair.com*, 10 November 2010, accessed 23 June 2011.

Safran Foer answers:

> This book is mine. His book is a masterpiece, this was my experiment. My story has nothing to do with his story. There's the sense that every book ever written is like this, if you use the dictionary as a starting point. This is a more limited palette, but it's the same idea.[16]

Placing Schulz's book and Safran Foer's book side by side one morning, I investigated Safran Foer's story, starting with his choice of words. I had a theory. With hindsight it is easy to find the Holocaust in Kafka. Perhaps Safran Foer found it in *The Street of Crocodiles*? Perhaps he had the story of Schulz's death, and the Holocaust itself, so firmly in his mind that he might have chosen to retain only words soaked in this darkness. I am still not sure whether this is true or not.

I did find that Safran Foer's new sentence structures always use words and punctuation marks from Schulz's sentences in the order of the original. The new 'sentences' of text may have large or small white spaces inside them.

The new structures, with their white spaces, sit alongside and in-between the physical holes made by the die-cut process. The content is, and at the same time is not, Schulz's content.

---

16 Safran Foer had obtained permission from Marek Podstolski, Schulz's nephew and the copyright holder of his estate, for his *Tree of Codes* venture.

Intrigued by this method, I experimented with choosing items from Kurtz's essay using the same rule: anything, from anywhere, as long as it is in the same order as in the original text. The muttering poem is the result.

At some point I stopped caring about the scholarly search for Kurtz's meaning and the method used by Safran Foer and started caring about the life of the new poems. I see these as my poems now, alive in the world, but having strong genetic links to Kurtz's essay. I do not know whether these poems succeed in locating what Glenn Kurtz learned from juxtaposing fragments of Sappho's poetry with his own grief and the general human process of mourning. I expect not.

A warning:

I must emphasis strongly one thing. All excavation is destruction. The archaeologist unearths a building, perhaps removing two or three later constructions in order to do so; its walls remain and can be seen or, if the wind-blown sand covers them again, they can be dug out a second time, but all the evidence given by stratification, by the position of objects, by traces of wood ash or by fallen brickwork, this has gone, and can never be recovered; he digs out a grave and all that remains is a hole in the ground and a group of objects in a museum; any evidence that he has failed to note has gone forever, and unless his record is scientifically complete he has defrauded science, and had better not have dug at all.

With this heavy responsibility he must be assured beforehand that he has a staff sufficient to do full justice to the work he would undertake.[17]

17 Leonard Woolley, *Digging up the Past: The Romance of Archaeology*, London: Pelican Books, 1937, p. 33.

In the summer of 2008, amongst a group of strangers roughly brought together, in a town that is part of New Zealand's gold-mining past, I met a man I had heard was a poet. A fog of awkwardness came up from the valleys and hung low over the table, causing the sound of our sips and swallows of tea to be magnified, as all sounds are in fog.

Pines from the northern hemisphere tolerate cold better than some native shrubs and plants, said one of the farmers at the table, and if they are not stopped they will eventually replace all the natives in the hill country. First you see a line of them, or maybe a plantation on a hillside. Then, if you look, you see a few in the paddocks nearby, maybe in clumps of three or four. If you stand still and look even further away, you can sometimes see a few moving, little Christmas trees, out by themselves, miles away from the original plantation. Like rabbits, he said. And then the conversation turned to the difficulty of killing rabbits in sufficient numbers to be useful.

Under cover of this conversation, I looked at the poet and asked him what had brought him to writing. He paused for a moment, perhaps considering how to answer this personal question asked by someone he had never met before. There was a time in his life which required everything of him, he said. He gave me sad details which I will not share here. Late at night, by the fire, after days that each lasted a hundred years, he began to write poems. It was the only thing which kept him sane, he said.

After this, he looked at me and asked what brought me to

writing. I told him that even though I had had an easy life, my reason was the same.

Later he wrote to me, sending me a book of his poems. I like poems that come from the heart, he said, in his letter. Some of our well-known poets write cold, abrupt, precise verse that I find hard to understand. I think those poems come from the brain.

He had lived his life in the high country, he said, in a way that has now almost disappeared. It was hard to explain.

He told me he had a disease of the eyes which meant that he could no longer read, and that although it might seem that this would be a terrible thing, in fact it was something which had liberated him from all sorts of obligations.

At first he had noticed that straight lines, such as the edge of a table or the top of a fence, looked wavy or crooked. Man-made objects looked further away or smaller than usual. After that he noticed that he could no longer see faces clearly. Finally one day a dark spot arrived in his central vision and had never shifted since that day.

He had been moved to write many poems in his life. At home I read all the books of his poems. I saw his first love, a woman with dark hair, who left him one day in a way for which he was not to blame. I saw tiny men and their animals moving across the land for reasons which could not be deciphered. I saw the sun rising and setting. And I saw a dark spot which covered almost everything.

Now again, grasses wave

mule trains
old tin huts
the southern cross
hanging just above the pines

night winds
frosted star

fragrance   tussock   ferns

wild swans, the cottage
lilac flowers in her horse's mane
but everything
sweeter than that

white faced cattle, that distant camp
signs, yes   I see the sunset
flaming like a bushfire

the saddle horse is standing   silent form

Keas call for me

as if searching for something that's missing
But I have not been back

her gentle heart, that old blue hill
a sapling willow that we planted
before the snows came down

splash of scarlet berries
thunder of night-rivers

but everything sweeter than that

I'm not sure what to call what I have done

When I describe it, other poets look at me askance.
I chose the latest collection by a poet who has written
hundreds of poems but has never hit the big time.
I read all the poems in his latest collection and I wrote down
only the *beautiful* words.
If it was music it might be called sampling.

As proxies for philosophers and people of all religions,
I asked four other people to read all the poems
in the latest collection by the poet who has written
hundreds of poems, and write down
all the most beautiful words.
Any word or phrase chosen by three or more of us
was saved.

As the person with the idea I claimed the right
to arrange these beautiful words into a poem,
leaving spaces to stand in for all the ordinary bits.

For a short time I was content with my new poem
and undisturbed by the thought of the beautiful words,
and the words chosen as beautiful by a minority,
mixing with all the ordinary words, in the original poems.

But last week, seeing that there was a full moon and many
stars, I took the latest collection by the poet who had written
hundreds of poems but never hit the big time
and I set fire to it on the beach.
Soon I will make a new poem
from the words that survived the flames.

I have not discussed all this with the original author[18] so I don't know how he would feel about what I have done. Also, if I began this conversation with him, he might notice a couple of unfamiliar lines and I would have to confess that two of the best lines come from other poets whose work I happened to be reading at the time.[19]

I understand that this latter action is not at all uncommon, especially among poets, because every writer is also a reader and of course the words that make the most impact are likely to be remembered. Some writers say that they are surprised to find these buried treasures in their poems, insisting that when this happens it is an accident caused by the activities of the subconscious.

In my case it was completely deliberate. I even looked up the lines to make sure that I was keeping the power of the original. One of the first people who saw the new poems said that the last line of 'Now again, grasses wave' had something of the feel of Sappho about it. Yes, I said.

I am sorry that other readers have not met the poet whose words I used as an instrument. If they had they might understand when I say that in some strange way the new poems invent and recount his entire life story. At first I thought this

---

18 'Now again, grasses wave' and 'Keas call for me' are, with the exceptions noted, made up of words from 'Blue Jeans', *Thoughts from the High Country*, Naseby, New Zealand, 1999.

19 'But everything sweeter than that' is from Fragment 62, Sappho, trans. Anne Carson. 'Thunder of night-rivers' is from 'The Mountains', by James K. Baxter.

resulted from a piece of communication from him to me and from me to him in an unnamed and mystical eleventh dimension; this process rather more reciprocal than traditional psychoanalysis. Later I realised that in choosing the poet's most beautiful words I had also chosen his packhorses, ready any day to cross any river.

Some friends have asked me how I would feel if someone used some of my text. This seemed a reasonable question. I offered a paragraph about the high country to Speight's brewery company. I forsaw interesting complexities of profit and disgust. However nothing came of my offer. A more authentic test would be if someone used text I had written without an invitation.

In physics there were once thought to be three dimensions: height, width and depth. *A rigid body* moving in these three dimensions of space was thought to have exactly six degrees of freedom. Using permutations of these dimensions people specified the de-formed position and new orientation of the body in relation to its initial position.

When Elvis Presley sang 'Blue Moon of Kentucky', written by Bill Monroe in 1946, in the Sun recording studio in 1954 or 55, the original waltz time changed to 4/4 time, the country-style accompaniment changed to electric guitars and the acoustics were given a particular boom. The anatomy of Elvis Presley's throat and vocal cords gave the song a particular sound. This sound gave a particular feeling to people hearing his voice. The song Elvis sang, which was the same as the original only in melody and words, is referred to as a *version* of Bill Monroe's song.

At that time the tradition was that people often made their own versions of songs they liked, and gave credit to the original songwriter. This credit took the form of written acknowledgement and money. Because of the degree of difference in tone between Elvis's 'Blue Moon of Kentucky' and the original, much gentler song, which could be compared with the difference between casual sex and lifetime love, some people thought that Bill Monroe would be offended by the Sun Sessions version. But Monroe sent Elvis a letter of thanks. This may have been inspired by the money he received from every purchase of Elvis Presley's version on vinyl. People may have liked Elvis's version better than Monroe's, but Monroe still owned the rigid body of the song.

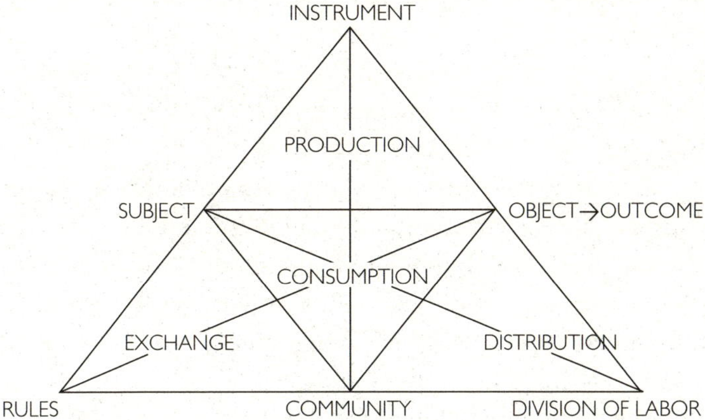

'The structure of human activity'[20]

20 Yrjö Engeström, *Learning by Expanding: An Activity-Theoretical Approach to Developmental Research*, Helsinki: Orienta-Konsultit Oy, 1987, p. 76. (It has been suggested to me that this diagram lacks sufficient context to be interesting or is ridiculously ambitious. I continue to argue for its relevance. I find its scope impressive and I like that it talks about money.)

Q: When was the golden age of thrifting records and why?

A: Dublab director Bryan 'Morpho' Younce:

For me it was the early to mid-nineties, when I first started getting serious about record shopping. I found a lot of great jazz and psych stuff in those days. People were still getting rid of their record collections because they all thought CDs were this great technology that was taking over for good.

A: Mark 'Frosty' McNeill (Dublab DJ):

Today! Hidden treasures are always out there. Someone's garage is being boxed up and hauled down to the thrift store at this very moment. Who knows what's in the back of that station wagon? The Out of the Closet thrift store chain is especially awesome because they're all over town and the records are only a dollar each.[21]

---

21 'Secondhand Sureshots: Each Snap, Crackle and Pop Tells The Story', *larecord.com*, 7 December 2008, accessed 28 June 2010.

Ras_G:

Secondhand Sureshots with me, my man J Rocc, Daedelus, and my man Nobody. They all my mans. It's a documentary put together by my man Frosty, lab rat cats over at Dublab. He gave us all 5 bucks, took us to Out of the Closet, made us buy 5 records, and he kept the records, it's not like we got to actually hold the records down and make beats on our own time, nah. They came to our house with the cameras, brought the records with them and recorded us hearing the records for the first time. I can't wait till it come out, when you see it peep it out.[22]

22 Sweenykovar, *Sweeneykovar.wordpress.com*, 29 October 2007, accessed 28 June 2010. This blog has now been deleted.

Thomas Brett:

The idea behind the documentary DVD *Secondhand Sureshots* (Dublab Collective 2010) was to invite four DJ/Producers to each build a new track based solely on their vinyl finds in California thrift shops. The DJs Daedalus, Nobody, Ras G, and J. Rocc would each have five dollars to buy any five records they could find (and which could not be previewed at the store). The rules for assembling tracks were equally strict. A track can only be built out of sounds sampled from the found vinyl, and only cuts and effects (reverb, etc.) can be added to the track. No drum machine beats, other instrumental sounds, or extra samples can be used in the compositional process . . .

When asked how he cleans his records, Ras says that no, no, dust is good: the audible crackling it creates functions as 'seasoning.'[23]

23 Thomas Brett, *Brettworks.com*, 11 February 2011, accessed 30 July 2012.

Thomas Brett:

After the tracks are finished they're mastered and pressed to vinyl and the DJs meet to listen to one another's work and share their vinyl finds. Meanwhile, a new piece of composite record cover art has been rendered from shards of the twenty LPs used to make the new tracks. Assembled onto one disc in this new composite record sleeve, the work of the DJs now forms yet one more piece of vinyl destined for . . . you guessed it, *the thrift shop*. And so . . . we watch Daedalus, Nobody, Ras G and J. Rocc return to the thrift stores and secretly drop off copies of their new creations into the dusty bins.[24]

24 Thomas Brett, *Brettworks.com*, 11 February 2011, accessed 30 July 2012.

Everyone knows that when a culture is in decline, or has been defeated by a greater power, its discarded artifacts float by themselves in the world, unguarded. Objects floating like this have no protection. They are available to be 'discovered' by others, sorted, uplifted, sold and resold until perhaps a select few reach a museum. Following this pattern, objects from New Zealand found their way to dealers and museums in Britain and Europe during the colonial period.

Right now, cast-away objects pile up on the pavement outside houses, in 'op' shops, on websites and in the tip. These might be objects valued by a previous generation, but almost worthless now, like my grandmother's crystal, or objects that never had much value to begin with, like cheap appliances and bedding found in skip bins at the end of the year when international students leave New Zealand to return home. Whatever you think about this, it is familiar.

But this final process of the *Secondhand Sureshots* project, where a new object made from old is placed back in the unguarded space of a thrift shop; *this* keeps me awake at night.

Lying in the dark, thinking of new but reconstructed objects in unguarded places, I find myself picturing a group of dark-haired young people in blue shirts, building a rough new wooden fort next to the memorial to the Warsaw ghetto uprising. As the sun goes down, they build a fire and most of them eat, dance and sing songs. A few of the young men and women carry weapons. They guard the fort from watchtowers.

The people I see in the night are young Jews, born everywhere, returning to Poland because they have been invited by a Polish activist who will soon be assassinated by other Poles. The return says that Jews and Poles can't do without each other after all.

All of this is part of an artwork by Israeli-born artist Yael Bartana, called *And Europe Will Be Stunned*.[25] After seeing this collection of three films at the Govett-Brewster Gallery in New Plymouth, I was full of something I could not explain to anyone.

Later I phoned the curator of the exhibition and asked her why the gallery had chosen to display Bartana's work and how the public had reacted to it in provincial New Zealand in the summer of 2012.

The curator told me of her longstanding interest in making exhibitions she described as politically engaged, and the commitment of the gallery to experimental and challenging work. Her answer set me to thinking about what makes a work 'politically engaged'. After a while I came up with a theory that political engagement might be as simple as noticing and mentioning something problematic or intimidatingly complex in a work of art, as opposed to not mentioning such things. Bartana's work goes much further than this. It takes a painful and unresolved subject and pokes a sharp stick into it.

---

25 *And Europe Will Be Stunned*, dir. Yael Bartana, 2011.

Sometimes you can find out what reviewers thought about exhibitions in galleries and in museums, and you can see when artists receive awards or criticism that catches headlines. You might read on line that visitors enjoyed an exhibition, or even that they didn't, but it is rare to see any mention of what meaning other visitors made of an exhibition. I would like to hear what other people thought Bartana's work was about. I know it might not be comfortable.

It's only a dead tree

Some friends who live in the same street as me are having trouble with a huge, mostly dead macrocarpa[26] which has its roots in their neighbour's place but hangs over their house like the arm of a crane, creaking and threatening to come through their roof each time there is a storm.

The problem is that the macrocarpa tree, along with several absurdly tall pines and a tiny roughcast bach from the 1950s, all belong to a woman who lives in New York. She is adamant that nothing at her Raumati property can be changed. The macrocarpa tree cannot be cut down. Nor can it be trimmed. Not by an arborist. Not at my friends' expense. And not because it might fall and hurt them or break their house in two. My friends are worried and exasperated. They have sent many emails to the woman in New York. They have had lengthy discussions with their insurance company, in advance of a likely catastrophe, and now the woman in New York has stopped answering their emails.

They are stumped. I am stunned too. They are such polite and reasonable people that I cannot imagine them failing to negotiate a resolution to this problem. Then I think about the woman in New York and I ask if they know why she is behaving like this about a dead tree. They say they do not

---

26 *Cupressus macrocarpa*. Naturalised New Zealander. Grows larger here than it does in other places. Can grow to forty metres high. Trunks of three metres diameter have been documented.

understand it either. After all, she only comes to the bach once a year for one week. Why does it all matter so much?

Then comes this extra information. Her mother came here after . . . they said. Somehow, from the pauses, I know they mean that the woman in New York is Jewish and that her mother was a survivor of the Holocaust.

From my imagination and from the accounts of other survivors who used to spend happy seaside summers at Raumati in the 1950s and 60s I guess that out here by the sea, the mother of the woman in New York and all her refugee friends used to sunbathe and relax with people who, like them, did not have family to visit, and like them, needed all the sun they could get. Maybe out here, at the bach, with the windows open and the smell of pine trees coming into the bedrooms, that little girl also had a rest from everything.

None of this helps with the tree situation.[27]

27 A friend who works in the museum industry told me that recently he revisited a museum he helped establish about ten years ago and found that absolutely nothing had changed from the day the museum opened. I am not expecting many changes to the tree situation either.

L-P 67[28]

]nd this overhan[

]tructive spirit [

] truly did not lik[

] and now because [

] the cause neither [

] nothing much [

---

28 Jim Powell, *Sappho: A Garland: The Poems and Fragments of Sappho*, trans. Jim Powell, New York: Farrar Straus and Giroux, 1993, p. 37.

9 February 2001: In a town called Drohobych in Ukraine, Benjamin Geissler, a German documentary film-maker, records the exact moment that Bruno Schulz's murals are found in a pantry off the kitchen of a shabby apartment occupied by Nikolai Kaluzhni, a former Communist Party clerk, and his wife, Nadezhda. The shabby apartment is part of a house occupied during World War II by Felix Landau, the Gestapo officer in charge of Jewish forced labour. In 2001 some people in Drohobych still call the house Villa Landau.

Schulz, known for his avant-garde writing and visual art, was required to paint on the wall of the room where Felix Landau's children played. This arrangement kept Schulz alive until November 1942.

Since World War II, others have searched for these murals, even searching in this same pantry, but until this day no one has noticed the shadows clearly visible under the painted surface of the walls in a place above the doorway. Encouraged by this, Geissler, his father, a camera crew and three Polish-Ukrainian art experts who have raced to the scene, squash into the pantry, looking past bags of onions, strings of garlic and the shelves of rags and pots which signal poverty in any language. One of the experts starts applying a solvent to the paint on the wall while all the others watch. Outside the pantry, and outside the shot, the former Communist Party clerk is in bed, dying of cancer, and his wife lists her illnesses and burdens in a language which might be Ukrainian or Russian, or Russian-influenced Ukrainian.

It is not difficult to find information about Landau. For one thing he kept a diary of his actions and feelings.[29] Of an early-morning execution on 12 July 1941, he wrote:

> At 6 a.m., I am suddenly wakened from a deep sleep. Fall in line for an execution. Alright, I'll play the role of the executioner and after that the gravedigger. Why not? It is strange. A man who loves to fight has to shoot up defenceless people. 23 are supposed to be shot . . . Strange, I am completely unmoved. No pity, nothing. That's the way it is and then it's all over... Valuables, watches and money are put into a pile.

29 Benjamin Geissler, 'Drohobycz', *Benjamingeissler.de*, accessed 9 September 2012.

At the time when the murals are relocated, Dieter, one of Felix Landau's children, is living in Australia. Christian Geissler, the director's father, phones and speaks to Dieter's wife in English. He explains that he wants to ask Dieter about the paintings by Bruno Schulz. Dieter's wife, who has an Australian accent, says that Dieter would not want to talk about this.

I find it somehow shocking to hear that Dieter Landau lives in Australia. I don't expect to hear these challenge-and-parry conversations from Australia, which is *over here*, not *over there*.

Some interesting negotiations must have gone on after that because next we hear Christian Geissler asking Dieter, in German, if he remembers the paintings. He doesn't. He was too young. He was only three or four. The list continues. He hardly ever spent time inside the house. He definitely doesn't remember the paintings. Then Dieter asks Geissler how old he is. Seventy-one, says Geissler. Well, says Dieter, in that case you know how crazy things were back then.

Agnieszka Kijowska, a member of the Polish-Ukrainian expert group, wets cotton wool with clear liquid from a bottle and wipes yellow-beige paint from the walls of a tiny room. As she wipes, the colour red appears from underneath.

> The festive red of sealing wax and calendar print, the red of coloured pencils and of enthusiasm, the amaranth of happy telegrams from far away.

Amaranth usually refers to a type of grain. But amaranth can also be a purple colour or an imaginary flower that never fades. I spend some time wondering if 'the amaranth of happy telegrams', from Schulz's 'Spring', might be something you could understand literally if you had lived in Drohobych in the 1930s. A reference to the colour of the type used in telegrams, perhaps?

We hear the voice of an older man, Mr Wojciech, who is obviously close by. As more of the top layer of paint comes off, we hear a conversation between Kijowska and Wojciech. This particular version of their conversation is transcribed from the English subtitles of Geissler's film *Finding Pictures.*[30]

Mr Wojciech: Do we know where this picture ends? Somewhere here?

Ms Kijowska: I don't know – I don't think there are distinct segments. No, it seems to me that . . . Maybe there next to the green . . .

Mr Wojciech: There –

Ms Kijowska: Perhaps further down.

Mr Wojciech: It is enclosed by a rectangular composition.

Ms Kijowska: I don't think these figures have a background – Yes . . .

Mr Wojciech: What's this? A mural or not? This uncovered surface shows nothing.

Ms Kijowska: Only blue showing through. Is that it?

Mr Wojciech: The entire height of the composition?

30 *Finding Pictures*, dir. Benjamin Geissler, Benjamin Geissler Filmproduktion, 2001.

Ms Kijowska: It's probably just a blue wall.

Mr Wojciech: I see. The height . . . about one meter.

Ms Kijowska: Ahhh (*a rising inflection that you might use with a child*) . . . Here's a little face.

Mr Wojciech: It's sky blue, right? We all agree. And on the sky blue . . . (*loud: a pronouncement*) There's a scene that's about 80cm wide.

A man's face appears from under the paint. He is wearing a blue helmet.

Mr Wojciech: An asymmetrical composition . . . (*same loud tone*)

Ms Kijowska: Mr Wojciech . . . here's a little face.

Mr Wojciech: Wonderful! Oh my God! It's typical. Oh my God! Isn't it? It's typical. It's reminiscent of his self-portraits. Oh my God!

Ms Kijowska laughs

Mr Wojciech: This is it!

Ms Kijowska: How true.

Mr Wojciech sighs

Mr Wojciech: Director, essentially this proves that it was Schulz.

He laughs

The facts of what happened in the days and weeks after that conversation are contested. The meaning of the events is even more contested. This version, part of a much larger article written by Celestine Bohlen, appeared in the *New York Times* on 20 June 2001.

> A bitter international scandal has erupted in a city in Ukraine, about 30 miles from the Polish border, where last month workers from Yad Vashem, Israel's main Holocaust museum, chiselled five fragments from a newly discovered series of wall paintings. They are the last known work of Bruno Schulz, a Polish Jewish writer, artist and Holocaust victim.
>
> With that single act, whose legality is disputed, Yad Vashem, the most august memorial to Jewish victims of Nazi slaughter, has unleashed a rumble of protests through a part of Europe that still feels battered and bruised by a vicious and violent century.
>
> The Schulz murals, illustrations of Grimm fairy tales that decorated the nursery of a Gestapo officer's son, have been caught in the throes of that history. According to Yad Vashem, the fragments in its possession, which depict a princess, a horse-drawn carriage and several shadowy figures, including two dwarfs, are now being restored. Plans call for them to be put on display at Yad Vashem's new historical museum in Jerusalem, which is to open in 2004.

The removal of the murals by representatives of Yad Vashem took Geissler by surprise. Celestine Bohlen describes the situation as Geissler understood it:

> He [Geissler] received a letter from Mr. Kaluzhni, dated May 17, 2001, saying that a group from Israel was ready to pay $3,000 for the murals, which, according to the city, had become his property through the process of privatization. In the letter Mr. Kaluzhni said he had refused the offer but two days later, the crew from Yad Vashem, led by a Ukrainian immigrant to Israel, arrived.

Geissler's film shows the pantry after the murals have been removed. Now there are irregularly shaped holes in the plaster where the murals used to be.

> The picture is destroyed, Geissler said [to Bohlen] in a telephone interview from Hamburg, and nobody will know the whole picture. For me, it is very tragic to see Bruno Schulz only as a Jewish victim or only as a Polish writer. He is simply Bruno Schulz, and this is a violent postmortem attack against him.[31]

31 Celestine Bohlen, 'Artwork by Holocaust Victim is Focus of Dispute', *Nytimes.com*, 20 June 2001, accessed 26 October 2012.

Between 2001 and 2008, the literary world in Europe and Israel expressed a range of views on what had happened, where the murals belonged and why. Often the reaction split along cultural lines. Poles: outraged. Ukrainians: also outraged but less noisily. A Jewish survivor from Drohobych, now living in Israel: initially amused, and then mentioning the word 'complexity'.[32]

In his film, Geissler interviews two elderly Jews who have remained in Drohobych. One man says he has stayed so that he will not be buried in Germany. A toothless woman, sitting in front of a sagging curtain and piles of books, says she has stayed to guard the remains of the Jewish culture of Ukraine. She speaks, without noticeable emotion, of her unsuccessful attempt to persuade the library at Lvov to make a designated space for Jewish books, and of her synagogue, which has been set alight four times in the last ten years by nationalist groups.

Jews in Israel do not understand why we have stayed here, she says. After this she recites a list of why Jews have stayed in Drohobych. Her voice rises and rises as she gives reason after reason. I did not really notice this list until the fifth time I watched the film, but now I regard it as one of the most significant and beautiful parts of the film. The more I believe that the woman's quest is doomed to failure, the more beautiful and significant the list sounds.

---

32 I notice the same reaction myself. Initially when I tell people the story, they laugh. Then there is a gathering in of the laughter and a silence begins.

Press release from Yad Vashem, 27 February 2008:

Today, Israel and Ukraine signed an agreement relating to the Bruno Schulz works located at Yad Vashem. The agreement was signed by Pinchas Avivi, Deputy Director-General and head of the Division for Central Europe and Eurasia in the Israeli Foreign Ministry, and Ukraine's Ambassador to Israel Ihor Tymofieiev, in the presence of Ukraine's Vice Prime Minister Ivan Vasyunik.

According to the agreement, the Schulz works, currently located at Yad Vashem, will be recognized as the property and cultural wealth of Ukraine, and will be on temporary loan at Yad Vashem for 20 years, after which the loan will be automatically renewed every five years.

Bruno Schulz was born in Drohobycz (then Poland, today Ukraine). A Jewish author and artist, he was forced to embellish with fairy-tale protagonists the walls of the children's room in a house occupied by Nazi officer Felix Landau. He was later shot to death by an SS officer on a day of pogroms in the city of Drohobycz, only because he was a Jew. Some 60 years after they were made, the works were discovered in a state of neglect and disrepair. Yad Vashem acquired the works, with the agreement of the family, in whose home they were found, and the approval and blessing of the Mayor of Drohobycz, and a team of experts brought the works to Yad Vashem in 2001. Since that time, they have undergone professional conservation to keep them in the condition in which they were found and to ensure that no further deterioration of the materials and colors occurs in the future.

I am reading about Lost Art.[33] After a while I notice that each time one author mentions an artwork lost in a war, the next paragraph is always a disclaimer about how the loss of people is more important than a lost painting or two. The author seems to be worried that talking about the art might not be morally legitimate. Reading this made me ask myself if I had spent too long thinking about the *murals* of Bruno Schulz.

33 Lost, Discarded, Missing, Rejected, Attacked, Destroyed, Erased, Shredded, Transient, Unrealised and Stolen Art, that is.

October 2013: Who was to know that a particular small room in Drohobych would explode as soon as it was opened? Since the explosion, and in response to it, Benjamin Geissler has made a new work called *The Picture Chamber of Bruno Schulz: The Final Work of a Genius.* This work is a virtual reconstruction of the way Schulz's murals looked in May 2001, in the pantry of the Kaluzhnis' apartment, after the murals were uncovered but before three were removed by Yad Vashem and five by the government of Ukraine.[34] When he began this work, Geissler says, he was in search of his own solution to deal with what had happened to the murals.

The Picture Chamber of Bruno Schulz: The Final Work of a Genius showed in Hamburg and Luxembourg during 2012. The after-image of the room, as it was in 2001, has now taken on a nomadic life. It could even come here, to New Zealand. I could imagine it at the Govett-Brewster.

When I first heard about this reconstruction, I didn't know what to think. I was struck by the fact that Geissler's holographic depiction of the murals had been taken to Germany, and in my head I heard the voice of the old Jewish woman who wanted to look after the Jewish heritage in Drohobych. But I also knew that Geissler himself had wanted the murals to stay in Drohobych.

34 Benjamin Geissler obtained permission from Marek Podstolski, Schulz's nephew and the copyright holder of his estate, for this work.

I was interested that the virtual work was now the only way that people could see the murals in something like the pantry where they were painted. These ideas went round and round in my mind for months. During this time I saw that one woman had written about the virtual work as a symbol of hope. She did not explain how exactly this piece of art symbolised hope but perhaps she thinks that reuniting all the paintings and the room in holographic form undoes the cutting and separation that happened in 2001? This seemed an absurd position to me.

I asked Geissler by email whether he agreed with this woman that the virtually reunited image offers hope for the future. He gave two answers, both quotations.[35]

'It was as if I were empty as I thought of the lost human race, and I was calm in my hopelessness.'

and

'Therefore the memory scarcely told me more than this and closed up again, and I was calm in my hopelessness, as if I had never experienced fifteen years of childhood, Sicily, Indian figs, sulphur, Macbeth in the mountains.'

I feel as though I understand this answer.

---

35 From *Conversations in Sicily*, by Elio Vittorini, published in 1941.

Ukrainian writer Yuri Andrukhovych, who is able to speak with topographical precision about Schulz and Drohobych, looks out from that room that had been a pantry to the corner of Mickiewicz and Czacki Streets, in November 1942. A man whose pockets are stuffed with bread crusts is lying on the ground, growing deader and deader as the days go by. A swarm of black birds keeps rising from a partly destroyed building nearby. Over and over again something agitates them, they rise, circle the dead man in the street and then settle again in the rafters.

*

THREE

Point Last Seen

At night, any and all contributions are justified

When I tell people that I am interested in the subject of missing people, everyone has something to say. They tell me about people who vanish every year while on an ocean cruise, people who have been missing for ten years but someone, maybe an obsessed police officer, now retired, or a mother, is still looking for them. They tell me about adopted children who have never found their biological parents, mothers who have lost their children, women who grieve for children they never bore and men who have lost touch with their children. They also tell me about invasions and theft and colonies and predators and diseases and the loss of generations.

Often the scenario they tell me about is one of which they have some personal experience, like the story told by a man who runs a museum dedicated to the Holocaust, who speaks of the empty chair at the dining table the day after his father died. The family stood and stared, he says. They had food but could not eat. No one knew what to do, until his mother told *him* to sit in his father's chair. Although he had worked in the Holocaust museum for a number of years, this particular empty space taught him something new about absence, he said.

Lost Luggage ***by Jordi Puntí*** is the story of a baby born in Franco's Spain in 1945 and raised by nuns. The nuns name this baby Gabriel Delacruz Expósito, which means Gabriel Foundling of the Cross. At that time it did not do to enquire too closely into the fathers. When Gabriel leaves the orphanage he earns his living driving a furniture van all over Europe. On his travels he fathers four boys with four different women, in four different countries, and although the mothers do not know about this for many years, he prevails on them all to call the boys the local version of the name Christopher. The boys have something else in common too. They all see their father jump into a furniture truck one morning and that is the last they see of him for a very long time.

One day, out of the blue, a policeman comes knocking on the door of Cristofòl, the Barcelona son.

I have two bits of news for you, the policeman says. One good and one bad. Which do you want first?

Cristofòl should not assume his father is dead, the policeman says. Just missing, for a long time.

The policeman seems to think Cristofòl should do something about this situation. Somewhat reluctantly, Cristofòl visits his father's abandoned apartment, and finds a small room full of clues about Gabriel's life, including the names of Gabriel's other three sons.

Shortly after that, the four men meet for the first time in Gabriel's still-life apartment. There it turns out that whichever city he was in, whichever mother and son he was visiting, Gabriel always arrived in the same way, wore the same clothes, left early in the morning summoned by the horn of the truck, and wrote the same sorts of sentimental but short letters after he had gone.

As well as being the story of the search for Gabriel, *Lost Luggage* is the story of four men who were once four boys containing almost identical feelings of sadness.

So here you have the Christophers – four sons of four sceptical mothers and one escape-artist father – trying to reconstruct an unknown past.

The Christophers think that if they could *make a single knowledge* out of all their fragments of information and experience, they would become brothers. The method they decide to use for this is to *speak* as one. One of the brothers explains this to the reader. As a reader I find the repeated first-person plural pronoun 'we' very unsettling. I am also intrigued by how something as small as a two-letter pronoun could cause such instability. Impressed by the apparent power of this grammatical act, I begin to wonder if it might help in my own situation.

Desperate to understand a certain set of events, hoping that a clump of knowledge would form itself from crumbs, I have been calling meetings of people I think might have something useful to say. People who, in the normal course of events, would never meet and never want to meet. Some of the speakers come as delegates, representing many others. Some, like me, are present as individuals.

This sounds like an orderly enough process, and at first it was. My guests would speak quietly to each other from behind their walls. Clearly none of them believed that any sort of consensus could be reached, but they stated and restated their positions in a gentlemanly fashion and I listened. A bit like a conference.

But things are diferent at night. I do not call these night meetings. In fact I often wish for silence. At night my guests are still polite but more is exchanged than in the daytime.

Sometimes one person speaks, and another says, yes, I know what you mean. Or one might speak and another might say oh, what a strange language you speak. A process has been set in motion; I can see that, and I probably would not stop it even if I could.

One night, after reading the first few chapters of *Lost Luggage*, I ask my guests this question: If a pronoun can make brothers from strangers, what else could it do? Could it construct something useful out of bits and pieces? Could it reconcile the irreconcilable?

This was the reply:

We live thousands of miles from each other in cities and mountainous areas all around the world, but we are willing to pool our information and our experiences for the benefit of science, they say.

We have been building this theory for years, starting in the 1970s with nothing but kindly impulses. This photograph is us when we were much younger; all plaid flannel shirts, round spectacles and muscly legs. How proud we were of that second-hand all-terrain vehicle. We paid for it ourselves.

These days, of course, we have long-term federal funding, every piece of geographical equipment we can think of and gleaming laboratories full of youngsters with PhDs in Bayesian mathematics.

In our country and in this time if a person disappears, you can 'report' the person 'missing', which means that the police will help you to find the person. They do this in a number of ways, one of which involves the use of specialist 'Search and Rescue' teams. I am very interested in these teams, curious about why people decide to do this work, and why people are prepared to pay large sums of money to fetch back human beings who have drifted, or even marched, away from the pack.

The place the person was last seen is the Point Last Seen or PLS. All calculations of the probability of finding someone in a particular area depend on knowing this.

I watch as many TV programmes about searches and rescues as I can.

Someone, a man or a woman or a visitor or a local or an older person or a younger person, is missed or is known to be in trouble. Someone, usually a friend, contacts the authorities and asks for help. Other people, mostly volunteers, go out looking for the lost person. The searchers leave no stone unturned. They tramp in the rain through bush, up steep slopes and along sharp ridges, they fly about in helicopters, leaning out of the open doors, peering into the night with heat-sensitive binoculars.

The searchers talk a lot about where the person was last seen, his state of mind and what he was intending to do.

They keep going with their search until either they find the person or they decide they will not find the person for a very long time.

If the person they find is alive, they tend his wounds. They crouch or kneel beside the person, leaning in and over him. The way they talk to him, reassure him, and make little jokes with him. What is that if not love?

After this, the searchers carry the person towards a waiting ambulance or helicopter. If you did not know the story, you would think they were brightly clothed pallbearers carrying a coffin.

Then the friends or the family or the rescued person say how grateful they are to the searchers. The rescued person smiles and looks fragile. On last week's episode a man who had spent two days lying in a river said it was 'pretty self-reflective up there' and another man found in thick bush said he found himself thinking that this was not a bad place to die.

It does not put me off that all these programmes are the same. If anything, I like them more because of that.

People who are truly lost and those who are missing behave differently. The stats tell us this. But that is no use at the beginning of a missing person incident, when you face the unknown. Taking this into account, we employ a broad approach, not limiting ourselves to any possibility, but being open to any sort of information that might be useful in guessing the actual scenario.

I am surprised and a bit embarrassed to say that I have had more than one experience of someone seeming to disappear on my watch. In one of these situations I cannot say that I did anything useful. In the other, I called the police to ask for help, but only after someone told me to. Unquestionably these experiences have sharpened my interest in departures, searches and rescues.

Some of you will be in the middle of a missing person incident at this moment.

If you are in the middle of a missing person incident right now, the conventional advice would be to contact your local police. Depending a bit on your life-style, you may believe the police can help with your problem and that you are entitled to use this resource. Contacting the police is often a good decision too.

We are sorry. We know you are looking for more straightforward advice.

In the interests of perspective I will add here that more than ninety-five per cent of people who are reported missing are found within a few days. Most commonly, missing people are found in a place with special meaning for them, often a place of peace and rest, and most commonly, although not always, they return or are returned, unharmed.

Of the remaining five per cent who do not return unharmed, some will have disappeared without meaning to; the whole thing making sense later when the person is found and the circumstances revealed. The missing person may have fallen, injured his legs and feet, had severe stomach pain or been unable to move because of a heart attack, some of these circumstances more life-threatening than others. A person who takes himself away to commit suicide, however, is reasonably likely to die.

I did not know any of these things at the time I called the police.

We find it useful to think of eleven possible scenarios:

Avalanche
Criminal
Despondent
Evading
Investigative
Lost
Medical
Near Drowning
Overdue
Stranded
Trauma

We could list these situations in order of frequency of occurrence, and in some ways that might be more useful. But each country is different, so we have stuck with the alphabet as an organising principle.

Note: We are always considering possible new categories. Overestimation of one's physical or psychological capabilities is one we are looking at this year.

That Sunday morning I knew only that losing a person is like losing your keys. You try to find them by remembering the last few things you did with them and sometimes that works. But sometimes all it does is leave you with a hole in your vision. In that hole there is nothing.

I told the policeman about the fight. I told him that you had been gone a Sunday-morning-sized piece of time, and that having carried out a grid search of the neighbourhood and my conscience, I was sure you had left. I told him that you might have gone to the shop for a paper, seen an empty big green bus stopping, and decided to catch that bus. I did not tell him that I could imagine you walking into the sea and I did not tell him that the words 'called away', in my handwriting, had appeared on a piece of paper beside my bed a few days earlier. I did not want him to think badly of me.

The policeman asked me what you had been wearing that day.

I told him that when I woke up, there was silence. There was also an empty teacup upside down on the bench.

He asked me if you had any identifying features.

I told him that yesterday I cut your hair with clippers while you sat on a chair on the lawn. I told him that you chose the number 2 comb because number 3 was broken. I told him I rubbed your head in circles, pretending to look for hairs that I had missed.

He asked me if I had any friends or family I could call. He asked me to sit down. That's when I realised that he knew where you were.

We look for any signs of what might have happened.

A sign often indicates the probable presence or occurrence of something else. But a sign can also be a gesture, a nod, a movement, a signal or even a wave.

We explained to the young constable that a cup, upside down on a bench, could be a sign. What of? he said. We explained to him that his question might be the most important question of all.

Floating in a pool of blue light was the husk of a man, watched over by a woman with tired eyes who said her name was Louise. The man was naked. A tag on his arm said 'Anon'. Louise asked if this was you. As much as this was anyone, it was you, I said. That was good enough for her. She changed the tag on your arm.

The moment when a searcher sees or touches the missing person is called 'Making the Find'.

Sometimes a competitive element creeps into a search, causing pressure on individual searchers to claim a find. We are currently investigating whether there is a link between never giving up and competitiveness. In the end we may have to accept a certain tendency to competition in the character of our searchers.

With this in mind, a searcher who claims a 'find' must provide evidence that he has found the physical being of the correct missing person.

Louise spoke with great calm. Most people think the best thing is for someone who is loved to come straight back to their life, because they are missed, but that is wrong.

It is a problem of time, she said, and of fate. When someone has been called away, they have been called away, and they should stay away until their fate catches up with them.

When the men found you, she said, you tried to fight them off with your long thin arms. So they backed off for a moment and did what they did whenever they didn't know what to do; they thought of their own lives and their fathers' lives. That's how they came to the idea that a grey-haired man might feel as if he were a boy again, lying still on the grass in the Sunday-morning sun.

They were not sure that you wanted to be found, Louise said, so they sent you and your fate away together for a while to sort things out. It seemed best for everyone. Louise consulted her notes. She told me the name of the park where the men had found you. She asked me if the name meant anything. I said it was your favourite park.

We always start at the Point Last Seen. From there we extend further and further towards where we think the person will be, often across rivers or mountains or decades. If we find the person, and we usually do, we call that a success, and we enter that into our records. But, as we are trying for something more complete than a statistical picture here, we feel obliged to add that what we find is not necessarily comforting.

The ventilator lifted your chest in perfect time. Waves passed and re-passed on a screen above your head. Louise said I could sit beside you. I reached under the sheet and took your chilled hand. Louise said I was welcome to talk to you, although no one knew where the words would go. She did not know exactly where you were, she said, or whether there was a sound connection between there and here. That's when I realised that you must be further away than the top of Mt Everest, because a dying man was able to call his wife by satellite phone from there to say goodbye.

Louise walked in circles around your bed, speaking softly to herself in single words. When I asked her what these words meant, she said each was the name of a substance you needed to have on board. I pictured you dark in the water like a wooden canoe, lifted and set down by deep ocean swells.

The standard of proof we require for making the find is high, and we make no apology for that. All sorts of sightings occur.

One of us saw a recently deceased friend by the shores of a lake.

We did not speak to him.

We do not know what he was doing there.

Your eyes were closed. I knew you were floating a long way from shore, lifted and turned by the swell. I knew there would be sunlight flickering through your eyelids. I saw the shadow of an albatross and blue and blue and blue. That's when I realised that you were travelling alone across a sea so wide that you might never come ashore.

I held your hand and kissed you. I felt a wild urge to tell you to come back. That everything would be all right. But I whispered only true things in your ear.

I don't know where you are, I said. But I am here.

One morning, which seemed no different from the ones before, Louise said it was time to see if you would come back. It would not be easy, she said. It would be a test of your will.

What ending are you looking for? I said, in your ear. There are places where the water rises into the shape of a mouth, I said. Whole canoes have been sucked under in these places. If you want to find land, you must open your eyes now and read the waves. Look for where the sea turns brown with earth washed out from a river mouth, I said. Search for shore birds. You will see many canoes passing and re-passing – these people are all watching you. Some of them are waiting to guide you in. Others are just interested in what you will do.

It is no shame to be lost. That's what we say.

I saw a tree trunk floating just under the surface, dark in the water like a whale, you said, on your first day back. Then, as I came closer, I saw two canoes lying silent and motionless in the water near a river mouth. Each canoe had a man inside. One man gave no sign of seeing me. The other pointed to the shore.

Last night the wall at the foot of my bed ran with writing in all the old languages and I knew what all the signs meant, you said on your second day back, seeming to draw strength from this.

After you came back you were, for a time, an object of interest among our friends and acquaintances. Did you see white light? asked a friend with cancer. No, you said. It was just like a light being switched off. Were there warning signs? asked a friend with high cholesterol. Yes, you said. There were a few.

There is plenty of technical literature on 'the management of missing person incidents', as they are called in the missing person trade. These texts share a certain ad hoc character. Some are published with spiral binding, suggesting practicality. Some are never published on paper but are available on the internet.

Lost Person Behavior: A Search and Rescue Guide on Where to Look – for Land, Air and Water, by Robert J. Koester, is my favourite of these practical guide books. If I lost someone again, I would like to think that a searcher would have read this book very carefully, long before the day he needed it, and have its logic of categories and their accompanying tactics ready in his mind.

Just last week, while watching *High Country Rescue* on TV, I saw *Lost Person Behavior* sitting open on the desk of the Search and Rescue coordinator. Later, while the volunteers were driving out to the PLS (Point Last Seen) I heard them chatting in the car about which category this particular lost person belonged to. The lost person had a mental illness, said one man. Mental illness is a trump category that over-rides other categories, he said. The other man said nothing for a while. Then he said if the lost man was a Despondent, they should start looking in the lake near where he was camping.

Mr Koester is clearly an extremely capable and compassionate man. He sees the small picture and the big picture, he is optimistic and at the same time he is pragmatic. Unfortunately, although he discusses the motivation of missing persons, he does not discuss the question of the motivation to search, which leaves me in the position of needing to make that up.

Initially we thought our task was to leap into the action and transform it with acts of sheer physical courage. We were naïve. We concede that. The further we have travelled with this work, the more we have understood that these are complex situations. Consider for example the differences between 'lost in thought', 'a lost cause', 'a lost art', 'lost knowledge', 'feeling lost' and being viewed by others as 'morally lost'. To be honest, some of our brightest mathematicians do not understand these complexities.

We still think it is our job to leap into the action but now we think that some of the time we also need to hold back and observe and try to find a pattern. We believe these opposites can be reconciled. Must be reconciled, in fact.

The number of books and online guides about how to disappear is surprisingly large, leading me to suppose that a number of people need advice on this subject. Usually the authors are men in their forties who have an excellent understanding of technology. They write with a sort of compressed urgency, as though they hope against hope that the reader, who is far too casual in these matters, will pay proper attention to all the advice and put each and every step in place correctly. If a person does this well enough, he will not be found. It is that simple. The steps themselves require so much planning that a person who was only half wanting to disappear would give up by the end of the second chapter.

So who might follow all these intricate instructions? I am interested in this question but the books don't interest themselves in reasons. They treat disappearing as something that some people will need to know about, like buying property for investment perhaps, and they don't talk about how a person might have landed in a situation where disappearance is the only sensible option.

And supposing that I followed all the advice and disappeared, what would that mean? This topic does not get much attention in disappearing books either. In three books there was nothing at all. A disappearance expert in a television programme made one use of the word 'margins', one each of the words 'solitude' and 'temptation' and one of the phrase 'old haunts'. Obviously this man had heard from beyond the wall. My guess is that he does not want to hear about solitude and temptations and second thoughts and has a policy not to take calls from beyond the wall, but somehow the odd one gets through.

We try not to concern ourselves with 'Bastard Searches'.

These searches take both Police and Search groups away from their proper work and force us to think about what is in the minds of our two least favourite groups in the community – criminals and teenage girls. A Bastard Search is neither a proper criminal investigation nor a wholesome and vigorous penetration of rough country.

In saying that, while some of those who disappear definitely are bastards and some are teenage girls who cannot get their own way, some are criminals or annoying teenage girls who are in deadly danger.

I have also experienced the half-disappearance and reappearance of a friend. His was a DIY disappearance, without the benefit of any books or paid consultants. At the time I lost track of him he lived in Mt Eden, with a woman he told me was the love of his life. Later he said that she was an alcoholic and that he had tried everything to keep her happy. He left the woman, his job, his friends and his flat and went to South Auckland, where he got a job driving a truck that picked up wheelie bins. He didn't change his name and he didn't set up any complex systems of mail forwarding or disguised internet addresses. He just left, and for three years, during his mid-forties, he didn't make contact with me or anyone from his old life.

Another friend and I used to meet in cafés and after we had drunk two coffees and eaten sweet cake, we would poke our tongues into the hole of the disappearance. He's the sort of person who could end up with his kneecap shot to smithereens, I would say, thinking of certain Colombian drug cartels.

At times, after he came back, my friend would talk about what happened. We used to talk every few weeks in those days – I never liked to leave it too long in case he disappeared again. Some days we would just talk about everyday stuff but other times he would come back to his point of departure, each time describing what happened in a different way.

It was strange, he said, but he didn't really remember how the idea started. He didn't remember finding it in a book, or noticing it in his path. He didn't remember how it moved towards him either. One day it was just there, in the front of his mind, all sharp edges and promises. All he had to do was accept it into his body. He breathed in. Straight away he felt it moving in his stomach. Each time he breathed out he felt that he was tolerating its presence a little bit better and within half an hour he noticed that he was comforted by its influence and pleasantly curious about what would happen next.

The first thing we say to people when we find them is 'There is no shame in being lost'. Then we say 'We all get turned around sometimes'.

After that we think about airways and bleeding.

The first thing he had to actually do was work out where he would go. That wasn't hard either. He had always belonged to two classes, the way some people have two nationalities, so he figured he would just return to something you did with your back. He wouldn't have to leave the country or steal the identity of any dead babies. He would just trade on the reluctance of his friends to leave the southern motorway.

One day, when I asked him outright what had made him decide to do this, he said it was a phase transition. 'When water turns into steam, that is phase transition,' he said. He also talked about old barns and the specific greens and golds of lichen. He advised me to spend a whole autumn afternoon, as he had once done, watching a wooden barn. For all sorts of reasons I didn't do what he suggested, but when I read W. G. Sebald's description of wild blue flowers growing over the ruins of a bombed German town, I thought I had started to understand what he had seen one day in some warm paddock. I haven't yet been able to make any connection between water turning into steam under pressure of heat and the gentle subsidence of a wooden barn.

My friend came back of his own accord, but in some ways he has only half reappeared. Twice in the last couple of years he has spoken about leaving the life he has now and living somewhere warm by the beach. He would work in construction, he says, finish reading the Western canon and eat fish he caught himself. There is never any mention of other people in his re-disappearing plans, although one day he said to me that he thought there was perhaps something missing in him. He had noticed it all his life, he said, this feeling that there was something he couldn't name, which everyone else could do and he couldn't.

After he came back, did you ever say to him, 'There is no shame in being lost. We all get turned around sometimes'? If not, phone him or text him now and say it. Both parts. It's very late, but it might still help.

I would be lying if I said that everything was down to her and the booze, he said one day. The booze took away someone I loved; someone who was, at the beginning, a comfort to me. But there were other things happening too. There was the job for one. It was fine getting the job. As usual I had papered over a few awkward patches in my CV because I thought I definitely had the skills they needed, or close enough that I could wing it.

So then I had the job.

No one said anything bad to me, he said. I was writing some pretty good copy, I put in the hours and I drank with the partners whenever there was a new deal to celebrate. They kept paying me and my name kept appearing on staff lists. But somehow the idea of me as a part of things just didn't ring true. I thought it would be different this time, but it wasn't, he said.

The thing is, a life is supposed be lived on bedrock and mine isn't. That leads to certain recurring patterns.

What else needs telling?

That a heavy feeling came over us sometimes when we were young.

That it could sometimes be ameliorated by the wearing of a cowboy suit.

And that although nothing compares with the sharp pleasure of being found, being there when someone is found, is not at all bad.

Last time we spoke my friend told me he had moved to Christchurch where he had a job in PR for a property development firm. Apparently the company expects to make a killing in the rebuild. According to him, business in Christchurch is flourishing now as long as you know how to play it.

Our meeting last night began on a formal note. I am deeply grateful to you all for answering my call for help, I said. Thank you for being willing to share such personal insights. I was often moved by your humility.

Despite all this goodwill on your part I notice that mine remains a separate voice. I would not call this a failure exactly, but I had hoped your voices and mine would join somehow – the moment of joining both a sign of and caused by the arrival of some new understanding. I hoped my tall thin pronoun would just disappear. I don't know how I thought that would happen exactly.

I am ready to acknowledge now that I greatly overestimated the tendency and capacity of knowledge to emulsify. Each little gobbet of knowledge does no more than adhere to other gobbets. For me, this tendency to adhere, while stopping short of the end result I had hoped for, is still an important finding.

What is a tendency? you asked.

A moored boat in an incoming tide will have a tendency to move closer to the shore, but its position will always be a reflection of a sum of forces, I said.

That'll do, you said.

*

FOUR

I ring the bell anyway

Rambly prose format

Thinking about waves

People who live right beside the sea, as I do, think about waves. You might dream of a silent and never-ending surge that lifts houses from their foundations and floats them out to sea. Or you might imagine a single wave, thirteen storeys high, arriving as thunder that never stops. You ponder which fate you would prefer. You compare the odds of the giant wave with the odds of being hit by a bus while crossing Lambton Quay. You find reassurance in the fact that your house has stood in its seaside location for fifty years. You try to convince yourself that you accept your fate, that you are ready. As far as I know, everyone thinks about giant waves in these ways but I don't know anyone who has done anything practical as a result of those thoughts.

*

If a wave the height of my fence came and I did not have insurance on my house, a radio, a torch and enough medication, canned food and water for three days stored in the garage, prudent people would be a little shocked and disapproving. A wave the size of a fence is not only a known risk, it is an imaginable risk.

*

The lexicon of risk is mostly mathematical.

Statistical probabilities:	Consequences:
Almost certain	Negligible
Likely	Minor
Possible	Moderate
Unlikely	Severe
Rare	Ruinous

Your eye hardly stops as you take in the probabilities. But then you get to 'ruinous'.

*

Over two days this winter, waves broke up and took away all the pieces of a fifty-year-old concrete boat ramp across the road from my house. Not that this process is new. Beside the boat ramp, in the 1970s, there used to be a surf club and a house. And a few kilometres south, where, in 1942, the US Marines practised landings for the Pacific campaign, I am told the sea has taken three rows of dunes.

When I saw the damage to the boat ramp I was surprised that it had happened so quickly but did not really think about it much until a few weeks later, when I received a letter from the Kāpiti District Council forecasting changes in the coastline over the next hundred years. A diagram of 'Coastal Erosion Prediction Lines' showed the sea lapping, or clawing, at my letterbox in fifty years. By then the sea will have taken a hundred metres of sand dunes, a row of several hundred houses, gas and water pipes, electrical cables and a tar-sealed road.

The thinking all seems very scientific:

> Coastal erosion prediction lines = LT + ST + SLR + DS + CU, where
>
> LT = longer term historic shoreline change
>
> ST = shorter term shoreline fluctuation
>
> SLR = shoreline retreat associated with sea-level rise
>
> DS = dune stability, and
>
> CU = combined uncertainty

Combined Uncertainty is scientific too, in its own way.

There continues to be much discussion among residents about whether this coastal erosion line is a likely scenario or only a possible scenario, this difference seen to have great significance for resale values.

*

When I read the council's letter, I remembered a man I used to work with in the insurance business, back in 2007. This man had spent the years since the Boxing Day tsunami in 2004 making mathematical models of the likely effects of tsunami of different sizes on Wellington's business district. When he talked at team meetings about his predictions, I used to picture us, leaning out the windows of our thirteenth-floor offices, watching with interest as Hokusai's great blue and white wave rolled in from the harbour and up Featherston Street. Thirteen storeys, I thought, would be well above anything messy that might be happening at street level.

*

From the vantage point of today, I have probably been wrong to worry about the threat of a single catastrophic wave. But, as it turns out, thousands of noisy brown waves, each just a little larger than they used to be, seem as though they might matter a lot.

Rats uncounted

These men with salty names were whaling headsmen on the Kāpiti coast circa 1842.[1]

Horse Lewis
Long George
Bill the Steward
Bloody Jack
Worser Heberley[2]
Black Murray
Flash Bill
Gypsy Smith
French Jim
Johnny Jones
Long Bob
Butcher Nott
Fat Jackson
Geordie Young
Geordie Bolts

This morning I was shopping in McLean Street, Paraparaumu Beach. The night before I had been reading about a whaling station near a pā called Te Uruhi,[3] which used to

---

1 Barbara Macmorran, *In View of Kapiti*, Palmerston North: The Dunmore Press, 1977, p. 46.

2 These days descendants of Worser Heberley use their whale-spotting skills to help count whales for the Department of Conservation.

3 In January 2013, when the scarred body of a whale was found on the beach beside the Paraparaumu Boating Club, local iwi named him Te Uruhi after the pā that used to be at that place.

be at the mouth of the Tikotu Stream, where the skate-park and the public toilets are now. The author didn't say when the pā disappeared but she did say that in the 1920s Tikotu Stream was diverted to allow development at Paraparaumu Beach and now runs underground through concrete pipes, as Number Two Drain.[4]

With this knowledge, I start to imagine a pā near a stream you could drink from and a whaling settlement in that place.

Driving along the coast this morning, I thought I would glance up from the road and see canoes and dinghies crossing back and forth to the island carrying vegetables or pigs and sheep, or cooking pots or nails or logs or rope. Every single object counted and precious. Rats present, but uncounted. Maybe, on the right day, I would even see the *Tory*, a ship with eight guns, which, on 16 October 1839, anchored at Kāpiti Island, before sending a small boat over to inspect the field of a battle near Te Uruhi. A nor'wester probably blew that day as it did this morning and as it does most days in October.

The boat party from the *Tory* walked north from Te Uruhi to the mouth of the Waikanae River where five hundred men women and children lived in the pā beside the river at Kenakena, surrounded by a mile of stockades. Surgeons from the *Tory* worked for several hours extracting bullets, binding wounds and setting broken bones. When I first

4 Macmorran, *In View of Kapiti*, p. 43.

read this account, part of me wondered vaguely why there would be more than one surgeon on a small ship in a small corner of the world, but another part of me felt warmed by this description of kindly men intent on healing the wounds of strangers. Barbara Macmorran, a great-granddaughter of Octavius Hadfield, the first missionary in the area, tells us the *Tory* was 111 feet long and 27 feet 'in beam' and was 'run on man-of-war lines'. She names the captain and the other passengers, including two surgeons and one naturalist and doctor.[5] She says that the vessel came here, bringing Colonel William Wakefield, 'to buy land for his brother Edward Gibbon Wakefield's New Zealand Company colonists, the first of whom were well on the way to New Zealand before the *Tory* ever dropped anchor in Queen Charlotte Sound'.[6]

---

5 Macmorran, *In View of Kapiti*, p. 41.
6 Ibid.

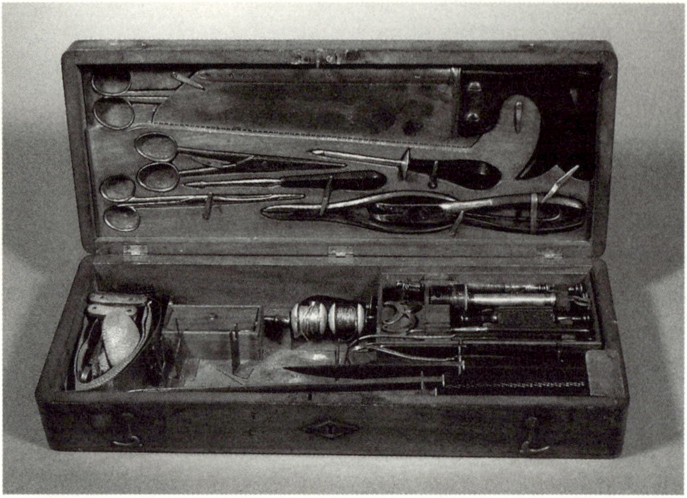

Surgeon's kit, circa 1830[7]

7 In the collection of Toitū Otago Settlers Museum.

Wakahuia Carkeek, a descendant of Te Rangihaeata, Te Rauparaha's nephew, also describes the *Tory* as 'sailing round the coast looking for suitable land [to buy]'. The *Tory*, he reports, was said to be 'carrying much merchandise as payment' and the Pākehā on board were 'keen to trade'.[8] In a chapter of his book titled 'The Problem of Land', he describes the disputes that began immediately after the *Tory* left.

Although she describes land sales by Te Rauparaha and consequent disputes in some detail, Macmorran does not single out the sale or loss of land by Māori as a theme, either as a chapter heading or in the index to her book.

A book is a series of decisions. Sometimes you do not realise you are making them.

*

A friend and I walked to the Waikanae river mouth last weekend. In the river right near the sea there are several small islands. We looked for a place big enough for five hundred people to live and we talked about whether the shapes of the islands, the wide flat channel and the smaller ribbons of water crossing the sand at the beach would have changed much in 170 years.

---

8 Wakahuia W. Carkeek, *The Kapiti Coast: Maori History and Place Names of the Paekakariki-Otaki District*, second edn, Auckland: Reed Books, 1967, p. 95.

Down on the beach that day a gale was blowing from the north-west. News of this wind had drawn kite-sailors from near and far. We stood for a long time watching these men who seemed to be standing on the water, joined invisibly to their sails, which were as brightly coloured as butterflies.

Looking back from the island

Kāpiti Island, after which the Kāpiti Coast is named, is a nature reserve administered by the Department of Conservation. The island's regenerating native bush is a place for reintroduced native birds to breed, but this can happen only if the island is free of introduced pests and predators. After decades of hunting and trapping, there are no more cats or possums on Kāpiti Island but rats and stoats are still a worry. Rats climb into visitors' bags and travel to the island by ferry. Stoats do that too, and maybe they even swim across from the mainland. No one is quite sure exactly how they keep getting over there, but they do. Once rats or stoats are ashore, they breed furiously. That is the problem.

*

Official documents describe Kāpiti Island as five kilometres away from the mainland, but in fact, it moves towards the mainland and away, according to its own laws and designs. It may, if displeased, pull away and make the journey to the mainland impossible, as it did for a week last winter, trapping a young woman who had an abscessed tooth. Or it may decide to come close, as it does in spring, because of its sympathy for young birds.

*

In the dying hours of a nor'wester which had turned the sea brown and made waves as high as a fence, I crossed to the island with twenty other people, including a woman from

Mexico who works as an environmental adviser to a German company trying to set up a coal mine on the West Coast, her mother who spoke only Spanish, a Māori chef from Otaki and two beautiful Japanese women who were on a summer holiday. Looking back from the island towards the mainland through binoculars mounted on a stand, we saw two men in a fishing dinghy in the distance, putting out crayfish pots.

*

Writing in a diary she kept between 1924 and 1942, Amy Wilkinson, wife of the custodian of what was then the Kapiti Island Bird Sanctuary, speaks of seeing smoke from summer fires on the mainland; bush clearances were a well-understood seasonal event in those years. I appreciate knowing that Amy Wilkinson witnessed that burning. That helps me to believe it really happened. I like hearing her voice too. From her diary I know she thought about the Pākehā hunger for land for more houses and the destruction of bush and I know she worried about the fate of native birds. But, although I know this is unreasonable, I want more from her diary of these years than the date of sightings of the Shining Cuckoo and the Long-Tailed Cuckoo. I want to know if she saw a Morepork in her kitchen on Kristallnacht or thought she heard the voices of women and girls singing, or anything else I could read as an omen.

And what the sky looked like on 27 November 1935, the night the first Labour government of New Zealand was elected. My father, aged nine, attended a party on that night, collecting signatures in his autograph book from men who would soon be cabinet ministers. 'Labour: the hope of the working man', wrote one of these men.[9]

*

On Kāpiti Island in 2012 we had a guide who said that she could talk about animals or plants or history, whichever we requested. I chose history, which was a minority choice, so most of the time, as we walked around the north end of the island, she pointed to trees and named them. She helped us to spot birds in the branches, and skinks, which live inside boxes used to trap stoats, apparently undisturbed by blocks of blue poison several times larger than their bodies.

We walked downhill along a path into denser bush with a dark canopy overhead. It was a little like walking into a tunnel. As I entered this place, I felt something which I can only describe as a separate darkness. I walked on, saying nothing about this feeling.

A little further on the guide stopped and told us this story:

> At dawn one day, spotters on the island saw hundreds of canoes leave from Waikanae and Otaki and paddle towards them. The water was dark with canoes so they knew a battle was coming.

---

9 I found this little autograph book again recently. As usual, I wondered if this man believed what he said and hoped against hope that he did. And, as usual, I couldn't throw the book away.

There had been warnings before this day came. The first was given by a party from Kāpiti fishing for hāpuku from canoes. Seeing another group on the water and mistaking this for a war party, they rushed back to Kāpiti to warn of an attack. After several days had passed, another food-gathering party crossed from Kāpiti to Paekākāriki to gather shellfish and karaka berries. At night, while they were collecting mussels, a war party surprised them and killed three people before the survivors could escape back to Kāpiti. This killing was the second warning.

A week or two passed. One night two children climbed a tall tree, looked out towards the mainland and saw hundreds of flickering campfires. Those fires were the third warning. It is said that later that same night a man from the war party crossed to Kāpiti and told the people on the island when and how the attack would be launched. That was the fourth warning. That man crossed back and joined the canoes in their early-morning attack.

*

Both the guide on the island in January 2012 and Wakahuia Carkeek, writing in 1967, say that Te Rauparaha and his men defeated this army of perhaps 2000 men on flat land near the lagoon at the northern end of the island.

Carkeek also tells of Hinewaioro, a Ngāti Toa woman who swam out to one of the canoes and captured a man she desired for a husband, and her father, who killed the 'handsome and willing prize'.[10] And of a Ngāti Apa chief, Te Rangimairehau, who pleaded not to be killed, but was 'hurled onto a fire where he was roasted alive'.[11] And of Te Aokaitu, tied up, taken to an oven and made to sing in the last moments of his life. Carkeek provides an English translation of his death song. 'One by one, those of that tribe who had been captured were duly consigned to the ovens,'[12] Carkeek says, making it clear that no other end was imaginable.

Our guide was more reticent. In fact she spoke in such a careful way about what happened after the battle that later I was unsure whether she said that the defeated men were eaten or not and if they were, why that happened and whether she had any opinion about this. I took from her reticence that this battle between people whose descendants still live nearby and the eating of one's beaten enemies are still subjects to be wary of.

10 Carkeek, *The Kapiti Coast*, p. 35.
11 Ibid., p. 36.
12 Ibid.

Hair

The concierge at my hotel in Sydney told me that although he worked just down the road, he would never visit the Jewish Museum because it was, in his words, too confronting. Inside, he said, there is a lampshade made of human skin.

Inside the museum, there is no such thing, but there is a blanket made partly of human hair. Apparently there are certain words which have the power to evoke the collective memory of the Holocaust[13] and 'hair' is one of these words.

There are two striped jackets like the ones you see in the movies, and some handmade wooden tools from the camps – a comb, a spoon and a knife. I had never seen these striped clothes up close before. The jackets were small. Through the glass case I could see the coarse weave of the fabric. There are photographs and maps and small cards explaining the objects. A comb was valued, it says, because keeping yourself clean helped you to avoid lice and that might make the difference between living and dying.

There are people in the Jewish Museum too. Some of them lived through the Holocaust. Some are the children of people who lived through the Holocaust. Some are visitors, like me. There is also a kosher café, which makes excellent vegetable soup, and a shop selling books and keyrings.

---

13 I use 'Holocaust' with a capital 'H' to show respect although the capital letter also makes me uncomfortable.

*

From my hotel room in Darlinghurst Road that night, I hear the voice of a museum containing objects that have survived the Holocaust of the Jews. Inside the museum there is so much pain, and also so much love and banding together. There is anger too. All this is held in place by steel walls. This is not a metaphor.

I want to open myself up to the voice of this museum and, at the same time, I am frightened of this place with its blanket and its striped coats. I wonder what will happen to me when I go back there in the morning and meet some of the people who work there and the survivor volunteers. To prepare myself, I practise sending parts of myself across the road, through the heavy doors and into the museum. I let them walk around a bit in the dark, and then I call them to see if they will come back. The first time I do this, all the parts come back so quickly that I wonder if they even went to the museum. I think perhaps they hid somewhere down the road in a café, waiting for me to call. The second time I send them, they come back but more slowly. I know they went inside the museum this time because of a voice which they bring back with them. It begins as I write the words 'objects' 'pain' and 'anger'. *Dein aschenes Haar Sulamith*, it says.

*

In the months since that night in Sydney I have begun to find those sentences about the voice of the museum rather ridiculous. I was away from home, I tell myself. I was by myself and thinking a lot about the Holocaust and therefore it would be quite natural to *imagine* a noise coming from the front of the building as if from a mouth and rolling across the road towards me in circles of dark grey heated air.

But last night, near the end of *Austerlitz*, by W. G. Sebald, I heard that voice again. In the midst of page 247, which I will admit I was reading rather dreamily, I found a description of Jacques Austerlitz searching for an image of his mother in some scraps from *Der Führer schenkt den Juden eine Stadt*, a Nazi propaganda film about Theresienstadt. By chance I turned on the television on 20 February 2012 and saw some of this film.

The version I saw had no soundtrack but it had late afternoon sunlight, just as Sebald says, and people tending vegetable gardens. One woman holds up a carrot, smiling and laughing as if she is proud of what she has grown. There are families where parents talk together and their children play nearby. No one is thin. I saw only one indoor scene – a barracks with bunks. In that scene a nurse, wearing a yellow star, spoke to a woman seated on a bunk. I think the woman might have been reading. Whatever she was doing, she sat awkwardly because the bunk above did not allow her enough space to hold her head up straight. A family sat at a nearby table. None of the people in the barracks looked sick. I did notice that the barracks was a place where many, many people slept. I found myself searching each scene for Austerlitz's mother, even though she is a fictional woman lost by a fictional man.

Austerlitz plays and replays the film. No matter how many times he watches the faces, looking for the mother he last saw when he was four, he does not see her. Desolate and desperate, Austerlitz finds a way to slow the film down to a quarter of its usual speed.

Everything is changed. People move as if asleep. Their eyes close and open in movements you might not usually see and when they walk they seem to hover slightly above the ground. The edges of their bodies blur and dissolve. Damaged sections of the film make strange patterns like drops of water under a microscope. A polka becomes a funeral march. A male voice, which had spoken before in 'high-pitched strenuous tones' of task forces and people 'willing to work' being 'deployed' in various different ways, became a menacing growl. The words 'menacing growl' made me sit upright. My heart beat faster than normal, as it does just after an earthquake.

At an earlier time, when I had considered making an attempt to describe the voice I heard that night in Sydney, I had been thinking of the word 'roar' but I had given up because 'roar' sounded like the sound in the story of the lion who lived in a meadow. I couldn't describe the depth of the bass in this sound and I couldn't describe a frequency that I heard with my old brain, not my cerebral cortex.

Sebald's attention to this noise reminds me that I have heard a menacing growl once before. Once, in a small town not far from where I live now, I knew a girl who had been kept as a kind of hostage for several weeks. One night, after reading and re-reading her statements to police, I dreamed of a huge flaming wooden wheel as high as a house, like a reel for electrical cables, rolling over paddocks and fences. This image was accompanied by a noise I have never tried to describe. I learned from this noise that the man had meant to kill the girl. This knowledge was something I never spoke of, knowledge of this sort slightly shameful to a person brought up in an atmosphere of light stained wood, plastic dinner sets and science.

Time is by far the most artificial of human inventions

Billy Pilgrim, the hero of Kurt Vonnegut's *Slaughterhouse Five*, comes unstuck in time. Billy can come unstuck at any moment. This is not the result of interference by aliens. It just happens.

The first time it happens Billy is a chaplain's assistant lost behind German lines during the Battle of the Bulge in 1944. While dying of the cold, he travels to the time before his birth and to the time of his own death. He would have liked to stay longer at his death time, bathed in violet light and vibrating, but instead he takes a long train trip in a boxcar, spends a little time in a prison camp, shelters in a deep cool slaughterhouse in Dresden while the city burns and then works in the hot ruins, accompanied by a few men and a horse. One of the men is a Māori prisoner of war.

As I write this I find myself inhabited by the tragic, laconic and simultaneously amused tone of Kurt Vonnegut. This tone is something Vonnegut brought home with him after his own experiences in the Battle of the Bulge and in Dresden during the burning. I'd love to know if, in addition to terrible memories, he brought back a diamond the size of a pea, like the one Billy Pilgrim found sewn into the hem of a coat the Germans gave him in a prisoner of war camp.

*

Karel Beran, another man in a boxcar, looked out at the city of Dresden twice from the top of a railway bridge. The first time the city was intact. The second time, just a few weeks later, another train stopped on the same bridge and again he looked out. This time nothing was standing except chimneys.

*

Sometimes Billy Pilgrim is an optician. Billy the optician lives in Ilium, New York, with a chubby wife and a small business empire. In that part of his life it is 1960.

In yet another part of his life Billy has been taken to the planet Tralfamadore, where he lives with Montana Wildhack, a mate the Tralfamadorians have provided, in a special zoo. Their house is a geodesic dome made to simulate a house on earth.

Outside the dome there is a guide who tries to explain some of the ways humans act and think to the Tralfamadorian visitors. One of the hardest things to explain is our earthling view of time. From the Tralfamadorian point of view every moment in time exists simultaneously, all the bad ones and all the nice ones, all the past and all the future, sitting right next door to each other like the high points in a mountain range. Knowing the past the future and the present, all at once, changes everything.

In spite of all their knowing, or perhaps because of it, Tralfamadorians do not *enjoy* thinking about bad moments. The night they bring Montana Wildhack to Tralfamadore is a bad moment for her, and she screams a lot. The Tralfamadorians consider this to be a terrible breach of manners, so they lower a curtain over the dome, as we might do with budgies in a cage if they were making too much noise.

*

There probably is no planet called Tralfamadore and no skinny man shaped like a Coca-Cola bottle with the name Billy Pilgrim. I know that. The trouble is that ever since I first read this book, in 1975, I have sometimes been able to see time in the Tralfamadorian way. Not only that but I find myself wondering how other people can ignore the Tralfamadorian aspects of places and situations.

*

Jacques Austerlitz, a fictional man in W. G. Sebald's book *Austerlitz*, who lost his family, his language and even his name, experiences time in a way which is equally as strange as Billy Pilgrim's.

Time, says Jacques Austerlitz, is 'by far' the most artificial of human inventions.

> The dead are outside time, the dying and all the sick at home or in hospitals and they are not the only ones, for a certain degree of personal misfortune is enough to cut us off from the past and the future.[14]

---

14 W. G. Sebald, *Austerlitz*, New York: Modern Library, 2001, p. 101.

Austerlitz finds that certain places have 'more of the past about them than the present'.[15] In those places, he feels 'the current of time slowing down' and that future and past events are all present. A person might feel, he says, that he has an appointment to keep in the past and that he must go 'in search of places and people who have some connection to us on the far side of time, so to speak'.[16]

In Paris, in 1960, Austerlitz boards with a Jewish woman near the Pont Mirabeau, but at that time he does not concern himself with her story, which was then from the recent past. Instead he studies architectural history.

In Paris at another unnamed time near the present, Austerlitz searches for his father in the streets near his last known address, always thinking that his father might emerge from some entrance and walk towards him. Austerlitz also sits in cafés and tries to imagine his father in those same cafés writing letters to people who never replied, or his father caught in the raids of August 1941 or July 1942, travelling through the Greater German Reich in his plum-coloured suit, now a little threadbare, and his black velour hat.

*

I sit upright and register the reference to the Pont Mirabeau, the bridge from which Paul Celan entered the Seine in 1970.

---

15 Ibid., p. 257.
16 Ibid., p. 258.

Speaking for those who were silenced

Akihiro Takahashi, a famous hibakusha,[17] died in 2011. He was born in Hiroshima in 1931. As a schoolboy he wanted to be a pilot. This is how he explains the fact that he stood still, looking up at the silver body of a plane flying low over his school in 1945. This particular silver body happened to be carrying Little Boy. The bomb exploded about two kilometres from where he stood.

Mr Takahashi says that he should have died that day. He saw terrible things. He spent eighteen months in hospital being treated for his burns, and was left with an arm that would not bend, fingers on one hand that could hardly hold a pen and chronic liver problems. In those days Akihiro Takahashi, along with the other hibakusha, was looked on as something not quite human.

*

I do not know what he did in the years after he left hospital, but I know that in these years he hated Americans and called the bomb 'an experiment' on ordinary citizens.[18] But then, in 1978, he visited Pearl Harbour where he met relatives of people who died there. After that he said 'it is important to transcend hatred, to transcend the agony, to transcend the sorrow'.[19]

---

17 Literally translated, the word 'hibakusha' means explosion-affected people.
18 'Voice for the Silenced', *Christchurch Press*, 31 December 2011, p. B13.
19 Ibid.

Akihiro Takahashi spent four years as director of the Hiroshima Peace Memorial Museum. There he guided visiting dignitaries and spoke to groups of school children. Over the years he told his story thousands of times. In 2002 he said:

> I tell myself that I'm a survivor of a terrible moment in history, and it is my belief that those of us who were saved should continue to talk of our experiences. We live to hand down the awful memories to future generations and represent the silent voices of those who died in misery and terror.[20]

Akihiro Takahashi had at least three lives. In the first he was a boy who wanted to be the pilot of a silver plane. In the second he was a man alive in hatred, agony and sorrow. In the last he was a man seeking to transcend the same things. Somehow it came to him that a man seeking to transcend hatred, agony and sorrow must pass on his memories and speak for those who were silenced. Perhaps one day, without meaning to conduct an experiment on himself, he just noticed that telling others something of his experiences left him with less hatred, less agony or less sorrow?

One article I read about Akihiro Takahashi mentions in passing a teardrop that may have rolled down the cheek of a man called Tibbets in 1980. Tibbets, a crew member of Enola Gay, the plane that dropped Little Boy, was sitting talking with Takahashi in Washington. That definitely

---

20 Ibid.

happened. The two men held each other's hands. That definitely happened too.

Then Akihiro Takahashi says he saw a teardrop roll down Tibbets' cheek.

Tibbets says there was no tear. He was sorry that people burned up down there, he said, but it had to be done.

I choose to believe Takahashi.

*

A woman who survived Auschwitz wrote in her memoir that after she became a guide at the museum and regularly told her story there, her nightmares became less frequent. But, she says, it may not be the same for others.

In America, Europe and Australia, museums to commemorate the Holocaust began to spring up in the mid-1980s, as never before. I have heard several theories about why this happened at this particular time. Some have said that the survivors were busy after the war, rebuilding their bodies, trying to find relatives, finding a place they could settle, making families and livelihoods. Only later, when this work had been done, could they pay attention to documenting what had happened. I think of them at this time as working their way *up* Maslow's Hierarchy of Needs[21] for the second time in their lives.

*

When asked, why talk of this now? some said the survivors knew that their own time was running out and they wanted to leave a lasting message to their children. Some had said very little to their children about what happened to them. Some had said a lot. Their children, at this time, were perhaps busy, enjoying the life that America or Australia had given them; not always keen on looking back through the black hole, to Europe. But they were maturing as their parents were ageing and their parents wanted to show them what they had seen and what had happened to them, while they could.

---

21 Maslow's Hierarchy is discussed in more detail on page 171.

The survivors also wanted to show non-Jews what they had seen and what had happened to them. They believed that if they said what had happened, and showed what had happened over there, people would understand Jews better and that would help to prevent anti-Semitism and racial prejudice of all kinds from taking power again.

There are many books written about this topic, but these ideas, which I read in the minutes of committee meetings, stand here as examples of the reasons for the establishment of museums dedicated to the Holocaust.

One woman, whose family contains several Holocaust survivors, told me that she thought Steven Spielberg's filming of 52,000 oral histories of survivors between 1994 and 1999 was a powerful factor in opening up the subject of the Holocaust. Spielberg, a wealthy and powerful American Jew who carried with him the authority of Hollywood success, gave these people a voice, she said, after the Holocaust had taken it away. After that, she said, they felt they had, for the first time, a mandate to speak about these events. I hear this as a cultural explanation, describing the meaning of Spielberg's enormous project to the Jewish population. You could also say that the construction of a huge archive tells everyone the topic is important.

*

Yesterday I read an essay in which Tony Judt describes the way each nation of post-war Europe has needed to forget the Jewish Holocaust at some times, and needed to remember it at others.[22] Language was always a willing scab in the cause of forgetting. These were not Jews, they were 'déportés' described on memorials as having 'died for France'. They were 'workers', they were 'victims of Fascism'; they were anything but Jews.

In Judt's opinion, certain trials in the 1960s, like that of Eichmann and of the Auschwitz guards, played a key role in bringing the actions of individuals to popular attention. Sometimes, he says, it was a new event, like the Six Day War in 1967 or the killing of Israeli athletes at the 1972 Munich Olympics, or even a television event, like the mini-series *Holocaust* which showed in West Germany in 1979, which brought the Holocaust of Jews to the notice of non-Jewish people.

*

In 1967, the year of the Six Day War, I wore out my first copy of *Exodus*. I cannot remember how this book, published in a distinctive bright-blue-covered paperback in 1959, came to me in Masterton in 1967. Perhaps everyone was talking about Israel that year, even in small-town New Zealand? Ari Ben Canaan, the soldier/farmer in his shorts and blue

22 Tony Judt, Epilogue, *Postwar: A History of Europe Since 1945*, London: Vintage, 2010, p. 803–831.

shirt, was my hero. I liked that his father carried his own brother over the mountains from Russia and built the kibbutz with its sprinklers and orange trees and argumentative violin-playing socialists. I liked that Ari was a reluctant soldier, wounded in spirit from all the fighting and dying. But I also liked it that he won.

When I think back to that time, I am dimly aware of newspaper headlines about famous Nazis being hunted in South America but much more aware of the arrival of television and westerns and the Beatles travelling to India and the first man landing on the moon.

I wish now that in 1970 I had known of the poems and death of Paul Celan who 'went into' the Seine that year from the Pont Mirabeau. But of course that is ridiculous. I had nothing to bring to those poems then and not for many more years.

*

I was here, in New Zealand, in the 1980s and 90s, beginning to read about the Holocaust, in the same period of time as the museums were opening and movies like Spielberg's *Schindler's List* were being made.

And now here I am, still in New Zealand, wondering if my writing is a sort of *automatic* writing generated by big swirls of events that happened in the 1960s in countries I have not visited.

More than a year ago a good friend, who speaks five languages and reads several more, told me it would not be possible to write about the Holocaust from New Zealand. There's so little to say here, she said. You should go to Europe.

But this is where I am, I said. That is the problem. This is where I am from, this is who I am, and this is where I am.

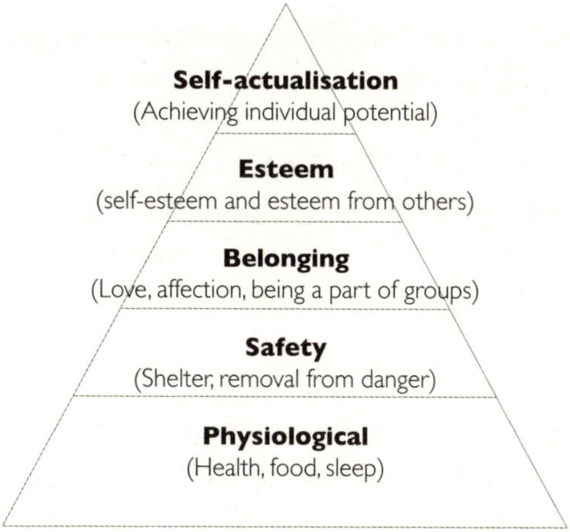

Recently I found this particular diagrammatic version of Abraham Maslow's 'Hierarchy of Needs'.[23] Abraham Maslow, the son of Russian Jewish immigrants, created the hierarchy in America during the 1940s to explain the conditions people need to be as happy and creative as they can possibly become.

Maslow's theory is that deficits in the needs on the bottom of the pyramid motivate human beings to try and satisfy those needs before meeting those on the top. The hierarchy works from the assumption that the needs lower down are more important than the needs higher up. Twice in the last year I have heard that listening to poetry was important to some

23 'Maslow's Hierarchy of Needs', *changingminds.org*, accessed 20 October 2012.

people in the ghettos but, past a certain point of hunger, nothing was as important as food. Behind the theory and the diagram there is a sense of instinctual striving from the bottom and the possibility of upward movement.

The hierarchy itself has been described in all sorts of ways and used for all sorts of purposes since the 1940s but it is always about people striving to make their lives better.

*

It is almost a convention for museums about the Holocaust to have dark grey walls. Often the Holocaust exhibit pathway follows the process of genocide in chronological order – it begins with identification, then exclusion and violence, proceeds to confinement in ghettos and concludes with the journey to a camp.

At the end of that journey there is immediate death by suffocation or selection for work, which meant slow death. Suffocation is so much the symbol of the Holocaust that sixty years later, members of a Nationalist group in Ukraine make a hissing noise when they want to threaten people by evoking this event.[24]

I notice that the process of genocide attacked the Jews from the top of the hierarchy – burned their art and books, locked

---

24 'Hooligans beef up for English football invasion', *Dominion Post*, 14 May 2012, p. B3.

them out of universities, and then took away their positions and their titles. Think of all the stories of doctors who couldn't practise and teachers who couldn't teach. Then it stopped them belonging to groups and alienated people from each other – neighbours who used to be friendly stopped speaking and people were driven to sending their children away or leaving old people behind as they fled. Then it proceeded to take down the formal and informal structures of law and safety. And finally, it took away their food and their rest and, last of all, their air.

There was no way for these people to come back. After the war, their neighbours said as much.

> we will not let you in
>
> this is our house now
>
> you were sent to a concentration camp,
>
> you were not expected to come back.[25]

Sometimes a museum represents this by making the physical space close in as the process nears its end. Sometimes the museum keeps shoes or spectacles or leaves as a symbol of all who died. The museums I visit all show that a tiny group of people survived, spread across the world, even coming this far, and that they wanted most of all to build families.

---

25 Moshé Liba, *The Holocaust – Between Me and Myself*, Wellington: New Zealand Jewish Chronicle Publications, 2000, p. 24.

The more I read, the more I think that we move forward too easily and not enough time and space and attention are spent on the deaths. Somewhere there should be rooms and rooms of total darkness, maybe an unbroken line of buildings three miles long, like the *Koloss von Prora*, Hitler's workers' resort on the Baltic, entirely made up of rooms of total darkness with one small room of survivors' stories at the end. Corridors could lead away from this small room to many other rooms, one bathed in fierce red sunshine for Australia and a tiny green and blue one for New Zealand. But this would not be a museum. It would be a three-dimensional story.

Increasingly, parallel with my reluctance to 'move on', I find myself wanting to know more of what was there before the rooms became empty and dark and how the survivors and their families lived, afterwards. Deborah Knowles, the daughter of a Holocaust survivor, is much clearer about why she feels this same desire:

> It is important for us to try to understand what Jewish life had been like before Hitler, so that it becomes possible to build a bridge over the void that divides the time before the war from after the war. Maybe then we can establish a sense of community and see ourselves as part of a group of people who lived before the Holocaust, who kept themselves alive during it and came out the other side.[26]

---

26 Deborah Knowles, Introduction, *Mixed Blessings: New Zealand Children of Holocaust Survivors Remember*, ed. Deborah Knowles, Auckland: Tandem Press, 2003, p. 9.

Belonging to the tribe

I came across Michael King's *At the Edge of Memory: A Family Story*,[27] at my mother's house. I inspected it.

The cover blurb of King's book described the book's content and likely appeal.

> A man turns up in New Zealand in the early years of the twentieth century, as if out of nowhere. He admits to no past, only to a present and a future; and he reinvents himself as a Catholic businessman. But the pressure of keeping a secret, of having to live with a repressed truth, eventually becomes too great. He disintegrates, emotionally and physically, leaving his family sparse clues as to his origins and identity.
>
> *At the Edge of Memory* will have a powerful resonance for all families whose ranks have been scattered by persecution or migration; it also casts a disturbing light on the specifically Christian ingredients of anti-Semitism.

The man who turns up in New Zealand is King's great-uncle by marriage. He lives his life as a businessman in Hamilton under the name Maurice Belgrave. As far as anyone knows, Bel, as he is known, never makes contact with his family back in Europe. My great-grandfather, who also popped up in New Zealand from Eastern Europe and settled in

---

27 Michael King, *At the Edge of Memory: A Family Story*, Auckland: Penguin Books, 2002.

Wellington, did not, as far as anyone knows, make contact with his family again either. This parallel intrigued me, as it had my mother.

King describes his book as a memoir. In the Author's Note, he explains his choice of the memoir form.

> Like so many true stories, and like life itself, the story [of the arrival of this stranger on a quest] has gaps that can be bridged only by supposition. Hence the memoir form in preference to conventional biography; and hence the title. The whole narrative arises from the edge of memory rather than from a central foreground of finely focused documentary evidence.[28]

I have been warned. I will not find a biography of Maurice Belgrave. I will find excavation of memory. If the life of Maurice Belgrave is found at all it will be near the place where memory turns into nothing. I am interested in this place. In fragments and supposition and white space.

I put the book aside to read in the evening. During the day I was occupied with 'A Report to an Academy'[29] (one of Kafka's short stories) and John Mulgan's *Report on Experience*.[30]

Franz Kafka's story was published in 1917, in German, in a monthly magazine called *Der Jude*. Martin Buber, a scholar

28 Ibid., p. 10.
29 Franz Kafka, 'A Report to an Academy', trans. Tania and James Stern, *The Complete Short Stories of Franz Kafka*, London: Vintage Classics, 2005, pp. 250–262.
30 John Mulgan, *Report on Experience*, Wellington: Victoria University Press, 2010.

of Hasidic lore and philosopher, who survived the Holocaust because he went to Palestine in 1938, was editor of this magazine. Kafka selected Martin Buber and this magazine's German-speaking Jewish readers as the audience for his story of an ape who forced himself to live like a man. This tells me that Kafka thought the story would speak in a particular way to these readers.

Kafka tells the story from the point of view of an ape, captured by humans, who learns to behave like humans. The ape has been invited to a learned academy to tell his story. Kafka's ape is very polite.

First he thanks the honoured members of the academy for inviting him to give an account of the life he formerly lived as an ape. Unfortunately, he says, he cannot provide that. 'I could never have achieved what I have done had I been stubbornly set on clinging to my origins, to the remembrances of my youth,' he explains.[31]

The ape did not begin with the goal of acting like a man. At first, after his capture, he sobbed hopelessly for his condition. But then he noticed that the men were free to move around while he was a prisoner. Aiming for even a limited degree of freedom, and with no promise that he would be treated like a man even if he acted like a man, he set about trying to do what men do.

---

31 Kafka, 'A Report to an Academy', p. 250.

One of the hardest lessons for the ape was learning to drink schnapps. I think back to the assimilation of Maurice Belgrave and wonder which part of life in New Zealand was hardest for him to learn.

As Mulgan says, talking of a time just before war was declared, 'You could forget Poland: it was a long way away.'[32]

Perhaps Maurice Belgrave 'forgot Poland', or whatever was his own Poland, for a long time.

*

Early in the book King describes the incident that caught his interest and triggered the writing of the book.

> Maurice and Margaret had in their household a woman named Annie Jones, nicknamed Ciss, who acted as housekeeper and child minder. In August 1943, Ciss had come upon Maurice in his living room. He was listening to a BBC radio programme with tears glistening on his cheeks. On air a journalist was speaking about Nazi extermination camps in Eastern Europe and the fact that the majority of inmates and victims were believed to be Jewish. 'Those are my people,' a grief-stricken Maurice told Ciss. He was already seriously ill, suffering as he had been for some years, from the effects of diabetes. Days after hearing the broadcast he was dead from a heart attack.[33]

---

32 Mulgan, *Report on Experience*, p. 75.
33 King, *At the Edge of Memory*, p. 27.

King hears about this incident from his mother and from that point on, he is interested in the idea that Maurice Belgrave was probably Jewish.

I started *At the Edge of Memory* at night, finishing it around 2 am. At 165 pages of text and 25 pages of photographs, it is a short book. I remember that, as I read, there seemed to be a veil between me and the heart of the story. I thought I could feel a heart there, under some layers. Sometimes I seemed to catch a glimpse of it, beating, but mostly I was unable to see it or feel its presence. That night I had a dream. Without the dream, I would have returned the book to the library, and thought of it as a story that never really happened.

Rather than forgetting the dream on waking, as I usually do, I found myself remembering it more distinctly as I set out on my morning walk. It seemed as though the act of walking in the cool morning air somehow made space for the dream, before the bright light and noise of the day could wash its colour away.

*

In the dream I was visiting or in some way amongst a group of brown-skinned people, living a certain way, under the leadership of a sort of guru. They all wore blue robes that fell to the ground. Their way of life was complicated – there were lots of rules and prohibitions. Their rules had one purpose, to make their lives gentle on the earth and on each other. I was my usual self, the way one usually is, in dreams.

For some reason I crossed into another group of people. Maybe I was just slow and was left behind as the others moved? Maybe I went away on purpose? These new people were tough and nasty. They had white skin. I took off my blue robes.

Without the blue robes I looked like these new people, or they looked like me, and I was able to move among them.

I heard them talking about their plan to attack all the blue-robed people and kill them. I went to warn the blue-robed people. I was amongst them when the killing started.

*

I started *At the Edge of Memory* again next morning, looking for connections with the dream. This second reading was a very different experience.

As I read the book this time I experienced an increasing sense of mistrust and unease at the actions of the author, which culminated in a rebellion against his power during Chapter Five, 'Voices from Europe'.

Everyone needs a handbag

I ring the bell anyway has already provoked different reactions from anything I have written before. The reactions began long before anything was written. Generally, when people ask me questions about my research and I answer, they fall silent. In Pākehā New Zealand, as on the planet Tralfamadore, a silence from the audience means 'Stop talking about this', or 'Stop doing this'. By continuing with this work despite these cultural warnings I have probably taken on some of the unattractive characteristics Reuel Anson Lochore described amongst the mostly Jewish refugees who came to New Zealand 'on account of Nazi oppression'[34] before the war.

> It is in social relationships that the refugees are weakest . . . . They lack discretion and tact. They revel in displays of emotionalism and self-pity, and fail to realize how we despise such lack of self-control. On social occasions, and other occasions too, they talk loudly and untiringly about their own affairs. Being bad listeners they cannot take a hint, nor sense an attitude from what we prefer to leave unsaid. . . .

34 Reuel A. Lochore, *From Europe to New Zealand: An Account of Our Continental European Settlers*, Wellington: A. H. & A. W. Reed, 1951, p. 73. Lochore's book began life as a paper for the government to use to assess the suitability of various cultural groups as immigrants to New Zealand in the early 1950s. Lochore is frank in his respect for people from Northern Europe and his disrespect for those from the South of Europe, and Jews. As the quote illustrates, his voice is clear and confident.

> so many of them in a very literal sense do not know how to behave themselves.[35]

At other times people bring up the well-known problems of writing about the Holocaust, as if I might not have heard of them or as if I should retreat in the face of them. The language people use for the risks I am taking shows that I am not merely risking artistic failure but also their personal contempt.

*

Thomas Keneally, an Australian writer of Irish descent, brought up as Catholic, might seem an unlikely author for *Schindler's Ark*, a book about a group of Jews saved from the camps by working in a fake factory during the war. Keneally thought this himself. According to Keneally's history of the book, the story of the Schindler Jews was sold to him one day in a handbag shop in Los Angeles.[36] The shop was owned by Poldek, a man desperate for an audience. When Poldek heard Keneally was a writer he said:

> I know a wonderful story. It is not a story for Jews but for everyone. A story of humanity man to man. I tell all the writers I get through here. Sitcom guys. Reporters for the *L.A. Times*. . . . you see everyone needs a handbag, everyone needs an attaché case. So I tell everyone I know the greatest story of

35 Ibid., p. 87.
36 I include handbags and briefcases and rucksacks in the category of 'suitcases'. See page 201 for a more detailed consideration of suitcases.

> humanity man to man. Some listen – an article there, a news item here. . . . But it's a story for you Thomas. It's a story for you, I swear . . .[37]

Keneally was looking for a briefcase, not a controversy. He had doubts about whether he should tell the story of Schindler and 'his' Jews, so many doubts that, in a separate book, he found it necessary to carefully spell out his rationale for persevering with the whole project.

One of Keneally's anxieties was that telling any Holocaust story that 'made it possible for readers to *imagine* the Holocaust, could be seen by some as an encouragement to Israeli hardliners'.[38] I find the logic of this quite difficult to understand, but have decided that he means that the more is known about the offences against the Jews during the Holocaust, the more violence by Israeli 'hardliners' against other people would be accepted or seem natural.

He finds a comparison in the question of whether stories about the Irish potato famine would inflame IRA violence against Britain. Then he mentions stories about the colonial settlement of Australia and their possible effect on Aboriginal people.

I am intrigued by these comparisons. My instinctive response is that I believe that all these stories of oppression should

---

37 Thomas Keneally, *Searching for Schindler: A Memoir*, Sydney: Random House Australia, 2007, p. 9.
38 Ibid., p. 125.

be told. I notice that Keneally went ahead and wrote the Schindler story and has written about the famine, treatment of Irish convicts and the treatment of indigenous people during settlement of Australia and subsequently.

But maybe he is right that scratching at wounds does not allow peace to grow? Maybe peace needs different words to be in the air, or at least the absence of too much repeating of atrocities?

*

Sometimes, when I describe my intentions for this project, people speak about the actions of the State of Israel in relation to the Palestinian people. I take the making of this link to be an argument that in the present situation, the Holocaust can, or perhaps should, not be talked about because of the continued suffering of the Palestinian people. Committed in my particular New Zealand way to the idea that we should act as though human beings are mostly reasonable, I do not, at present, believe that either one of these topics must make the other invisible.

Later, after *I ring the bell anyway* was mostly written, I came across a discussion between Khalil and Farouq, two fictional characters in Teju Cole's *Open City*, who complain that the Holocaust suffocates and deafens them when they try to discuss Israel's treatment of Palestinians.

> It's true, Khalil said. Europe is not free. The rhetoric claims freedom, but only the rhetoric. If you say anything about

Israel, you have your mouth plugged with the six million. You're not denying it, I said quickly, you're not actually questioning the figure, are you? That's not the point, Khalil said, the point is that it is against the law to deny it, and that it is also against an unwritten law to even bring it up in discussion. Farouq assented.

If we try to speak to the Palestinian situation, we hear the six million. The six million: it was a terrible tragedy, of course, six million, two million, one human being, it's never good. But what does this have to do with the Palestinians?[39]

The six million suffocate and silence Khalil and Farouq with their sheer numbers. I have no trouble believing the particular way the Holocaust acts for them after experiencing the way it acts in reverse. But I am left unsure whether they would like to 'deny it' if they could, and if they would like to argue for a smaller number if it were legal to do so. Khalil and Farouq's discussion moves then to a rejection of the Holocaust as 'unique suffering'.

*

As it took shape, *I ring the bell anyway* irritated some readers because it did not provide the gas chambers and piles of bodies which they expected to be at the core of any writing about the Holocaust and I, the author, seemed insufficiently undone.

---

39 Teju Cole, *Open City*, London: Faber and Faber Ltd, 2011, p. 122.

*

I also know that this work repels some people and makes others feel guilty. One man, a close relative, told me that he knows he 'should' read it, but he doesn't want to because he doesn't want to have the Holocaust in his mind. He has done whatever was necessary to avoid this pile of paper 'about the Holocaust' which has entered his house.

Another unrelated man said my work made him feel guilty about how little he is doing to help people who are being oppressed now. Others said that as they were reading, they wondered what they would have done to help if they had been alive in those times. I notice that no one imagines himself a Jew in those times.

Anglo-Celtic eyes

Researching his own memories as a context for Maurice Belgrave's abandonment of his Jewish identity, Michael King searches for anti-Semitism in New Zealand and finds it.

In Chapter One, as the mystery of Maurice Belgrave's life is being laid out, King's mother says that the New Zealand Maurice Belgrave/Moshe Belgoraj arrived in was anti-Semitic or at least xenophobic and so creating a new identity was understandable. She reminds her son about the furriers she worked for as a young woman and the 'sharply derogatory'[40] comments staff made about them based on their Jewishness.

In a rather disingenuous[41] device, King has his mother remind him about *From Europe to New Zealand: An Account of Our Continental European Settlers*, a book by Reuel Anson Lochore. This book, King says, revealed 'prejudices' about 'New Zealanders of non-British origin, especially those of Jewish descent'.[42] These prejudices, King says, were 'representative of those held throughout the country at the time' (the 1950s). King describes Lochore as:

> a retired diplomat who had taken me under his mentorial wing in the mid-1970s, when I had embarked on a career as

---

40 King, *At the Edge of Memory*, p. 28.
41 King had written about Lochore in some detail in *Metro* several years earlier in 1991.
42 King, *At the Edge of Memory*, p. 29.

> a fulltime writer. He was erudite, with degrees in languages, literature and philosophy; and he was kindly.[43]

In Chapter Two, King retells a story a priest told him. The priest's father always dressed up for the local A&P show as 'Ikey', a man in robes, with a long nose. King concludes:

> There was no racial malice involved – simply an assumption that this was what Jews looked like, and that they were different and amusing in Anglo-Celtic eyes.[44]

I react immediately and adversely to this sentence. I do not find this Poverty Bay Shylock amusing and I do not buy King's verdict that there was no racial malice, which I would call anti-Semitism, involved. As he says this I realise that I do not have 'Anglo-Celtic' eyes, or at least not in the sense he means.

In the next paragraph King tells us that this same priest talked to him about finding *Protocols of the Elders of Zion* in the seminary library. This book, as King says, 'was a notorious forgery by the czarist secret police designed to discredit Jews and add momentum to anti-Semitism in Russia'.[45] I notice this title as I would a gunshot, and after this I read even more closely to see who touches *Protocols of the Elders of Zion* and what they say about it.

---

43 Ibid.
44 Ibid., p. 40.
45 Ibid.

I see that King and I agree on the need for this analysis because he points out that there was no note with the book in the seminary library to say that it is a notorious forgery. King distances himself from the book by saying this, although in fact I have never seen a note in a book warning readers that it is a forgery or that it may incite hatred. The priest, who has spoken about the book and whose father dressed up as Ikey, is left in a more ambiguous position.

In later sections of this chapter King recalls a time when he was fourteen and he heard a man call a girl a 'greasy little Jewess'.[46] The man who said these words was 'a respectable Wellington businessman, a good family man and generous contributor to community projects who had served in the Second World War'.[47]

'*Who*, then, were the anti-Semites?'[48] King asked himself when he was fourteen, following this question to the possibility that here, in New Zealand, there might be people who condoned or even supported what Hitler had done. The young Michael King was, in his own words, 'astonished', 'appalled' and 'struck dumb'.[49]

King says that learning of the extermination of European Jews, during his childhood, with all the associated images from the camps, affected him profoundly:

---

46 King, *At the Edge of Memory*, p. 44.
47 Ibid., p. 45.
48 Ibid., p. 46.
49 Ibid., p. 44.

> At this time I lost the ability to laugh at any joke, however harmlessly intended, that poked fun at or caricatured Jewish behaviour.[50]

My distrust of King as a narrator of stories touching the Holocaust began in Chapter Two over the problem of how all the pieces fit together: all the statements of sympathy, amusing Ikey in Gisborne and the 'kindly' author of *From Europe to New Zealand: An Account of Our Continental European Settlers*, and *Protocols of the Elders of Zion* in the seminary library.

*

In Chapters Three and Four, King visits New York and meets David Belgray, a psychoanalyst who has devoted his life to finding and reconnecting lost members of the Belgoraj family. David Belgray's path to all this began with his uncle Manny, who 'used to recite the names of our grandparents and our aunts and uncles in an almost biblical fashion, who begat whom and so forth'.[51] As a young man David Belgray associated this recitation of genealogy with visits to the apartments of old people and strange cooking smells. But, eventually, he wanted to know what it all meant.

By the year 2000, when David Belgray phoned Michael King, he had been on this quest for about 45 years and had

50 Ibid., p. 46.
51 Ibid., p. 64.

compiled a family tree with more than 1200 names on it and another 1000 waiting to be entered.

For David Belgray the important thing was that these people had always felt as if they were 'remnants of a small clan dispersed by the Diaspora and ravaged by the Holocaust', but they could now see themselves as part of 'a large, living and loving family with a rich cultural heritage'.[52] It was good for people to feel this, he believed. It might even be good for King's health, he says, to see and experience something of the culture in which Bel had grown up. David Belgray dresses King in a yarmulke and sends him on his way to a synagogue to soak up some old-world Jewish atmosphere.

King enters an ultra-orthodox synagogue in Borough Park, Brooklyn, alone. 'It might as well have been another planet', King says of the scene which greets him.[53] Sounding like a lone Englishman surveying a tribe of natives, King describes his impressions and his plan:

> I understood neither the forms nor the content of these complementary forms of worship and reflection. And I did not seek out anybody to interpret for me precisely what was going on, for two reasons. One was that I did not want to impede or interrupt the participation of any member of the congregation. The other was that I had not gone there in an analytical or anthropological frame of mind. I simply wanted to see, hear

52 Ibid., p. 76.
53 Ibid., p. 79.

> and experience forms of ritual that would have been part of my great-uncle's shtetl upbringing.[54]

At first, King, the outsider, is ignored except for some hostile glances from a group of young men. But when he starts writing notes an older man comes over and says quietly that King should not write during the service. He is welcome to stay and observe as long as he obeys their customs. King apologises and puts the paper and pen away.

After this a number of men of about his own age come over and sit with him for a few minutes. They ask him, in a friendly way, why he is there. King tells them about his search for understanding of his great-uncle's decision to come to New Zealand and to change his name and identity. They are interested in his search and tell him about their own searches and their links to particular shtetls, but there is a big difference between Maurice Belgrave's story and theirs. Their families have maintained their Jewishness and they are proud that so much of European Jewish culture from before the 1930s still exists in their part of America.

But then Judah, a man in his fifties, comes over and begins 'what felt like an interrogation' about King's reasons for visiting. 'To my shame', King says, 'I decided to tease him, curious about what that might bring to the surface.'[55]

---

54 Ibid., pp. 81–82.
55 Ibid., p. 86.

A religious debate follows. It ranges testily over several issues before Judah says that it is possible that assimilated Jews caused the Holocaust. Perhaps if they had stayed in the Jewish world and not been so visible, Christians might not have been provoked into attacking them? Perhaps God produced the Holocaust because so many Jews were abandoning their laws? These are views which must be considered, Judah says.

King disagrees with this, and says so, firmly, calling Judah's question 'wrong-headed and brutal'.[56]

Judah accuses King of cultural tourism. King feels uncomfortable and leaves. I am also uncomfortable, but I do not leave.

*

In Chapter Five, King interviews Erna Winton, an elderly Jewish woman who is Moshe Belgoraj's niece. Throughout this chapter King takes up a sort of commentary position, as he did in the synagogue in Chapters Three and Four, but this time it feels more critical. Parallel with this he describes his own actions.

*

---

56 Ibid., p. 89.

According to King's account of what happened, he phones Erna (that is her Australian name) from his Melbourne hotel room. She is deaf. He asks if he can visit her. She says he can come the next morning. He arrives at the house. He points out that Erna's front path is overgrown with weeds.

Erna does not answer the door when he knocks, so King bangs on the front door with his fist. When she appears down the side path, he tells us that she says the word 'wait' as 'vait'. She has rolled-up rugs behind the front door and he has to push really hard to open the door, he says.

According to King, Erna is delighted to have the chance to tell her story. No one has asked her to do that before, although Spielberg[57] has already collected her husband Rudy's story because he was in the camps. King points out her German way of pronouncing the name Spielberg, and then he lets her start.

She is young and beautiful. More beautiful than her sister. She is clear about this. She plays the violin and has ambitions for a career in music. She and all the other young ones are modern and cultured. They speak German. The old ones are devout and scary. They speak Yiddish. There are fields of wheat and peasants, wolves, of course, and snow. The old man, Moshe's father, has a whip. Two of his sons go to New York to get away from him. One of those sons goes as far as Hamilton, New Zealand, where, according to family rumour, he had black children.

---

57 She means through the Survivors of the Shoah Visual History Foundation.

Erna's story promises to be interesting, with a grim old man and his runaway sons as the researcher's treasure and her own story, the one she knows best, as a bonus. But I never really get to hear her story because King, the author, stands between me and Erna, getting in the way all the time. Sometimes he is just there, occupying space that I wish Erna was occupying. Sometimes he makes comments from the side about Erna, telling us that she is suffering somewhat from dementia, or that in his opinion she *was* beautiful. I get fed up with this.

I quit as the compliant reader of his book. I begin something new. Whatever it is that I am writing it will have different rules from this book.

*

I write a play. I call it *And also it was cold there in the winters.* In the play, nearly everything is exaggerated.

King appears as a sort of Kafkaesque judge, with Erna his target. The rugs, the weeds, the shape of her nose, her accent and her claims of past beauty are her crimes. Everything she does makes her guilty of being old, from Europe and a Jew. I take pieces of Michael King's text to use as his voice. This seems fair.

I appear as a somewhat violent person who is very touchy on the subject of the Holocaust. I warn King that he is being judgemental about Erna. I ask him nicely to let Erna speak. He does not change his approach, so I gag him with a clean white hanky. After that we all sit still and listen to Erna's story for as long as she feels like telling it.

Erna appears as an elderly Jewish woman with two names. Erna is her Australian self. Esther is her Jewish self. She has lost many of her family and spent nearly fifty years married to a man who was in Dachau and Buchenwald and lost nearly all his family. She is still beautiful and exactly as crazy as everyone else.

She is a bit deaf to New Zealand Anglo-Celtic English, but hears perfectly in German, Yiddish, Hebrew, Polish, Russian and Romanian. She talks for four hours in English, with the occasional word of German and Yiddish thrown in as delicious seasoning.

Mostly she talks about herself. Where possible, I use her words from King's book. Sometimes I have to guess what she would have said, based on bits and pieces that King mentions but does not elaborate on.

This is what I add. There are plenty of wolves and sleigh rides and Erna has a valuable violin because she deserves it. There are some anxious and hungry years during the war and just after in what was then the British Mandate of Palestine. There is a search for family left behind in Europe and many letters from the Red Cross which make her cry. There is a romance with a man who dresses well but is alone in the world and then two suitcases and a ship which docks in Melbourne.

My version of Erna's story and King's are not always interested in the same things, but at one point in King's story, and in mine, Erna says that her mother knew her brother Moshe Belgoraj, as she called him, was in New Zealand and wrote to him in 1938. She received this answer from his wife:

> My husband does not wish to communicate with his relations. Please do not attempt to contact him again.[58]

Erna's mother believed her and never tried again. Erna also tried to contact the family in the 1950s or 60s while she was on holiday in New Zealand. She phoned a Belgrave from the Hamilton directory, she says, but the man told her he hadn't heard of her and hung up.

*

In the book and in the play Erna dies a few days after King's visit. On the day of his visit no one knows that she will die so soon.

58 King, *At the Edge of Memory*, p. 100.

Home

When I was first starting to learn about the Holocaust, I remember being preoccupied with the problem of how I would know when it was time to leave New Zealand. I would read about people whose lives were deeply rooted in a certain place in Europe. More deeply rooted than mine felt. I saw pictures of these people, captured in a moment in 1932 or 1936, by street photographers, as they walked in pairs along a street with a German name. So stylish. So confident-looking. This is *Before*. Sometimes *Just Before*, like the photograph of Paul Celan turning to look behind him in Czernowitz, in 1937 or 1938.[59]

I do not mean to suggest that these photographs lie. These people did walk arm in arm and the sun shone on them. Their clothes *were* more stylish than ours. If you look, you can even see hard times in the background of the photographs, like one I saw yesterday, which showed a woman in a dark-coloured coat with white plaited detailing and a feathered hat, striding along a street in Czernowitz. She is looking straight ahead in a rather fixed way, which may or may not be related to the fact that she is walking past a boy with ragged pants and no shoes, standing in a doorway.[60]

59 John Felstiner, *Paul Celan: Poet, Survivor, Jew*, New Haven and London: Yale University Press, 1995, p. 9.
60 Marianne Hirsch and Leo Spitzer, *Ghosts of Home: The Afterlife of Czernowitz in Jewish Memory*, Berkeley: University of California Press, 2010, p. 69.

But by the time of this 1937 or 1938 photograph Paul Celan had already transferred from one high school to another because of anti-Semitism. He and his friend liked to lie in the shade of a tall tree reciting Rilke to each other, but they never went far because that would have been 'too risky for two Jews in Romania of the 1930s'.[61] In 1938 Celan left for university in Paris, spending money his father wanted to spend on the whole family's emigration to South America. The young Celan's train, full of all sorts of people, passed through Berlin at the moment of Kristallnacht.

> *you caught sight of some smoke*
> *that was already from tomorrow*[62]

*

Before [*nice* pictures]

During [not the same person, shaved heads, striped clothes, thin bodies who could be anyone]

After [normal-looking people or wild, saddened people]

It's another of those set pieces.

*

61 Felstiner, *Paul Celan*, p. 9.
62 Paul Celan, *Gesammelte Werke*, ed. Beda Allemann et al., quoted in Felstiner, *Paul Celan*, p. 11.

As a younger person I spent time looking at *Before* photographs trying to see if *they* knew it was time to leave.
I thought I would see a darkening in people's faces, or perhaps an expression that said they knew it was already too late. But I didn't. Or maybe I did, but I didn't recognise that expression.

'Backshadowing' is one word for what I was doing, reading the past backwards, and using this information to 'judge the participants in those events as though they too should have known what was to come'.[63] I find myself guilty of asking these questions: Should they have known? How could they not have known? And, at the same time, who could have guessed?

'Paranoid reading',[64] a term used by Eve Kosofsky Sedgwick, speaks to my eagerness to *find* violence and danger hidden in these photographs before violence and danger reveal themselves, if they are there at all. If I find the bad stuff before it finds me, I cannot be taken by surprise. Paranoia is anticipatory, she says, and also 'tends to be contagious'.[65]

---

63 Michael André Bernstein, *Foregone Conclusions: Against Apocalyptic History*, Berkley: University of California Press, 1994, p. 16.

64 Eve Kosofsky Sedgwick, 'Paranoid Reading and Reparative Reading, or, You're So Paranoid, You Probably Think This Essay Is About You', *Touching Feeling: Affect, Pedagogy, Performativity*, Durham, N.C.: Duke University Press, 2003, pp. 123–151.

65 Ibid., p. 126.

A tchemodan

As far as I can see nothing answers the question of how Jews were supposed to know when it was time to leave Europe. I think this unanswerable question is the reason that I, a full citizen of New Zealand, have inherited a sensitivity, common among Jewish people, to suitcases. The ones I notice most are leather, or brown cardboard, made to look like leather.

1. Ernst Toller, a left-wing playwright exiled from Germany in 1933, had two suitcases. I don't think they would have been leather.
2. Michael King's great-uncle by marriage, Maurice Belgrave, also called Moshe Belgoraj, began in business by taking two suitcases of fabrics, buttons, needles and thread onto the Auckland to Wellington Express and selling from the aisles. These would definitely have been made of cardboard.
3. Rose Ausländer, a Jewish German-language poet from Czernowitz, only owned two suitcases in her life. They are in a museum now, in Düsseldorf.
4. Jacques Austerlitz had a canvas rucksack, which he describes as 'the only truly reliable thing'[66] in his life. Sebald provides the reader with a picture of it.
5. I'm sure I heard that Jews living in Germany since the war have an expression which means 'living on top of their suitcases'. It does not matter what these are made of.

---

66 Sebald, *Austerlitz*, p. 40.

6. At the Wellington Holocaust Research and Education Centre I saw thirty important books set out on a table. One had the word 'suitcase' in the title. Two had images of suitcases or rucksacks on the cover.
7. A Jewish man arrived in Australia after the war with only one cardboard suitcase. His friends laughed when they saw that the suitcase was full entirely of books in Yiddish. *The Communist Manifesto. Anna Karenina.* One suitcase and he could be at home anywhere. Home enough, anyway.
8. The newly relaunched Holocaust Centre of New Zealand now has two suitcases amongst its displays. One belonged to a man who, as a child, was sent away on the Kindertransport trains. This leather suitcase was the last thing his mother gave him. Inside the suitcase she had placed a list of every item of his clothing. Recently this suitcase attended a seminar to mark the anniversary of the death of Primo Levi, occupying space in the front row, alongside members of the diplomatic corps.
9. There is a stack of old brown suitcases outside a junk shop on Highway 1 just south of Otaki. Recently I felt obliged to stop and photograph it.
10. There is an old leather suitcase on a table outside a junk shop next to the Raumati Social Club, near my house. There are also several in my garage.

If only it were possible, I would get into the photo

In an empty apartment in Barcelona four fictional men searching for their lost father lay out all the photographs he has ever sent to each of them, hoping to find clues about their father's life. Added together, the photographs say a lot.

Afterwards, one of the men makes the comment that photographs only make sense when you already know the story.

Another of the men insists that this sentence be recorded: 'The passage of time always distorts reality.'[67]

*

For Marianne Hirsch, one of the most potent objects in the story of her parents' survival is a tiny photograph (1 by 1.25 inches) of her parents, taken by a street photographer in Czernowitz. On the back of the photograph, her father has written 'Cz 1942'.

Marianne Hirsch and Leo Spitzer, both eminent scholars, interrogate this photograph. Her parents' outfits, their facial expressions, their body language, their level of nutrition, the buildings in the background all attract their attention. They compare the photograph with others from the Warsaw or Lodz ghettos. They consider young love

67 Jordi Puntí, *Lost Luggage*, trans. Julie Wark, London: Short Books, 2013, p. 40.

as a resource. They consider her parents' commentary on the photograph – 'Here we are during the war' – and their description of their 'relatively lucky circumstances'.

After this they interrogate history. The date the Czernowitz ghetto opened. The date of its closing. The numbers of Jews deported in 1941. The waiver that saved her parents from that deportation. The deportations in 1942. The rules for the wearing of the yellow star. How big it had to be. How it was attached. All these matters attract their attention. Official records and survivors' accounts also provide some answers.

But they want the photograph to 'reveal itself even more',[68] so they make a digital scan of the 1-by-1.25-inch photograph and blow it up to about 4 inches by 5.5. Now they find a blurry spot on the lapel of Carl Hirsch's jacket. Is it the outline of a yellow star? But weren't stars bigger than that? Could her parents have been walking openly in the city in 1942 if they were marked as Jews? If it was a yellow star, why did her mother not have one on *her* coat? Was the spot a mark left by stitches after taking *off* the yellow star?

But stars were fastened with a safety pin.

If her father had taken off the star to hide his Jewishness, how did the couple feel about having their photograph taken in the main street? Did they buy the photograph only

68 Hirsch and Spitzer, *Ghosts of Home*, p. 164.

in order to take away the evidence of their presence on the main street that day?

On one trip Hirsch and Spitzer travel to Czernowitz with Marianne Hirsch's parents, who have not seen this city since they left it after the war. When they refer questions back to her parents, some doubt emerges about the date on the back of the photograph. Their final investigation of the spot on Carl Hirsch's jacket is reflexive. Here the authors describe their own 'desire, if not need, to penetrate more deeply into a world that had been opened up to us ever so slightly'.[69]

I notice that in his memoir, *Tales of Love and Darkness*, Amos Oz, whose father and mother arrived in the British Protectorate of Palestine in the 1930s, has written his own interrogation of photographs from before the war.

Oz begins with the sentence, 'A battered photo album survives from Vilna days.' He goes on to describe these inherited photographs. There is his father in school groups, there is his father with David, the brother who stayed in Vilna and did not survive, and there is his father at seventeen.

Which of the boys with the caps survived? Oz asks. And what of the girls with dark hair and berets? Which of these girls survived and which were starved and frozen and buried in pits in the Ponar forest? What is the meaning of a certain smile on the lips of some of the girls? Was there a day when

69 Ibid., p. 166.

a certain child in a certain ghetto hid underground and survived as a result? *Exactly* what decisions did each person make and how did each decision turn out? Oz notices family resemblances, and expressions of cheerful optimism. He notices clothes.

Hirsch and Spitzer's interrogation of the ghetto photograph is obsessive and insatiable but calmly described. That mixture is its power. Oz seems initially to be less interested in the physicality of the photographs. He is painfully explicit about the likely fates of these children and his examination of photographs finishes up with his own helplessness. These are his particular reactions as a writer and a man to looking at the photographs. But in the end, just looking at the photographs does not satisfy him either. He wants to cross into the world of the photograph and take action, even if that action would be futile.

> If only it were possible, I would get into the photo and warn him and his cheerful chums. I would try and tell them what's in store. It's almost certain they wouldn't believe me if I told them: would just make fun of me.[70]

70 Amos Oz, *Tales of Love and Darkness*, trans. Nicholas de Lange, London: Chatto & Windus, p. 99.

More awkwardness

Last week I found that I was talking with a woman of my own age, from my own country, but whom I don't know very well, about the Holocaust. She started the conversation by asking about a trip that I was about to make. Her question added a small risk of social difficulty to our conversation, as questions do. I could have answered this question in a general or evasive way but I chose in that moment to describe my intention to visit museums in Australia and New Zealand which have Holocaust exhibits. I added a thousand times as much risk of social difficulty by choosing to say that, and it is a measure of this woman's character that she chose to join me in the conversation.

A conversation like this is always a bit uncomfortable. Sometimes silences occur in these conversations which no one knows how to end. One of these silences grew between me and a German friend in 2002 and it has not been broken yet.

Last week's conversation went quickly to a bus tour this woman had been on which included Auschwitz as part of the package. She told me about her visit to the Jewish Museum in Berlin, which reminded her of Te Papa, and where, she felt, the building overwhelmed the objects. She also told me her impressions of the stone fields of the *Memorial to the Murdered Jews of Europe*. She told me about height as a carrier of meaning in this memorial. In some parts of this field of stone plinths you can see people walking around and in other parts, as the height of the plinths increases, the people disappear. She believes that this capacity to make people disappear is the point of this monument.

After a few minutes of descriptions of heritage sites and monuments, she stopped talking and looked away, downwards and to the right. After just a minute, the woman raised her eyes and looked at me again.

'I remember how shocked and surprised I was when I met a woman at work whose parents had both been . . . you know . . .' she said.

That these people had been in concentration camps. That is what she didn't say. When I first wrote about this, I felt confident that I knew what she meant. She meant, and all this would have rolled off my tongue without hesitation, that she grew up in a country where she felt almost completely safe. I interpreted her unfinished sentence as a measure of the gap between her life and that life.

*

If you asked my colleague, now, if New Zealand really was as safe as we felt when we were young, she would say yes, for her, it was. Her adult self will know that not everyone in that country at that time felt as safe as she did, but I bet that when she thinks of her own childhood, it is a place of lamb chops, vegetable gardens, school milk, school journals and worries a person could live with. This picture of our bountiful nutrition is not a figment of my imagination. Just this morning I read that in 1936, Sir James Parr, who had recently retired as New Zealand High Commissioner in London, told a League of Nations meeting in Geneva that according to the latest year's figures, New Zealanders ate, per person, an average of 37.7 pounds of butter, and a staggering 236 pounds of meat. Coming just a few years after the Depression, this was a matter of pride. Italians at the same time ate 2–3 pounds of butter and 35 pounds of meat.[71]

*

I thought that the shock and surprise this woman felt when faced, in Wellington, in 1978, with survivors of the Holocaust, was caused by that bounty of milk and meat and the blueness and roar of the Pacific Ocean, known to drown out almost all other sounds.

*

When this woman and I were children in the 1950s and 60s, the War, as people called it, already seemed like something that happened a long time ago. Our parents spoke of it, but they seemed to be living with us, in the present. If, like our family, you had no direct connection to the people who died, perhaps the news of what happened in Europe really would take thirty years to arrive in New Zealand? I wonder if, despite constant reminders from the Jewish community, the news will ever really arrive?[72]

*

---

71 Vincent O'Sullivan, *Long Journey to the Border: A Life of John Mulgan*, Wellington: Bridget Williams Books Ltd, 2011, p. 169.

72 A non-Jewish reader told me recently that this question is too highly charged. I think Jewish readers would find it absolutely reasonable.

A choice my great-grandfather made in 1878, to come to New Zealand, kept his descendants safe. We do not know the names of his relatives or even where in Eastern Europe they lived – there is no one left now who knows these things. We know he started his new life in New Zealand quickly by marrying a Jewish woman and making a large family. For whatever reasons, Isaac (that was his English name) did not apply for New Zealand citizenship for fifty-odd years, which meant that in the late 1930s, when Jews everywhere worried about their safety, he was not a New Zealand citizen.

I have sometimes imagined him listening to the radio, hearing about the Nuremberg Laws or Kristallnacht – things of little interest to most New Zealanders at the time, but much talked about in the Jewish community. Once I went as far as to imagine a whole play in which he receives a letter late in 1938, from a sister, telling him how and when his parents died, where they are buried, and asking him to sponsor her son and his family to come to New Zealand. She doesn't care about herself, his sister says, but he should help the children if he can.

In my play Isaac raged and cried and banged his walking stick on the wooden floor and told no one about the letter, not his children who were first cousins of the son back in Poland, and not his wife. I was never very clear about the reason for his rage. Perhaps he was angry because he was ashamed of not having money to help? Perhaps he was angry because he thought he had left his family far enough behind that no claims could ever be made?

Whatever his reasons for delay and then for action, he lodged an application for naturalisation on the 25th of February 1938, eighteen months after the passing of the Nuremberg Laws and nine months before Kristallnacht. I know, because I have seen the document with its official stamp, that a Member of Parliament provided a character reference for Isaac to use in his application for New Zealand citizenship. The reference describes him as 'indigent' but of good character. I try on the idea that the Member of Parliament was a person for whom my great-grandfather had once made suits. I see Isaac with a tape measure around his neck, kneeling on the floor in his shop in Upper Cuba Street, beside a rather portly ruddy-faced man wearing good-quality tweed. I also try on the idea that money changed hands. However it came about, late in life my great-grandfather became a Jewish New Zealander, on paper as well as in his life. His children were already Jewish New Zealanders and their children were Jewish New Zealanders too; well mostly anyway.

*

In a fictional scene in a book set at Otago University between 1932 and 1935 Dan Davin, a New Zealand-born Catholic writer, has his protagonist Martin Cody challenge a New Zealand-born Jew about his politics.[73] The Jew is a conservative, on the side of the government against the hunger marchers. Hitler is the real enemy of the Jews, Cody

73 Dan Davin, *Not Here, Not Now*, London: Robert Hale & Co. / New Zealand: Whitcombe & Tombs Ltd, 1970, pp. 301–302.

says, not the Communists, and if things don't change all the Jews will be dead. Overall it's a morally confusing scene in which Davin allows Cody to know the future and say wise and worldly things to Werner, a naïve New Zealand Jew. Cody dislikes Werner, and the reader knows this. But Cody needs Werner on side in his quest for advancement, so he sets out to flatter him and pretends to befriend him. Werner, who, like Kafka's ape, has a dreadful need for acceptance, falls for it.

Leaving all this aside, I am most interested in a comment that the New Zealand Jewish character makes. 'Being a Jew doesn't matter in New Zealand', Ben Werner says.[74] This is a very simple sentence but its meaning is not obvious to me. It might mean that Werner does not see his future life as constrained by anti-Semitism as it would be in Europe. It might also mean that holding on to Judaism itself is not important here. This one comment, written perhaps in the late 1960s, filtered through the eyes of a Catholic New Zealander living in Britain, is all I know of the views of Jewish students at Otago University between 1932 and 1935.

*

In the Jewish community a lot has been said, and continues to be said, about assimilation as a threat to the existence of the community in New Zealand and elsewhere. I have heard it said that in New Zealand we have a set of factors which are particularly potent in producing assimilation. Remoteness from

---

74 Ibid.

other Jewish communities. The small size of the community. The high rate of intermarriage. The lack of Jewish education. There may be other factors too, which I am not aware of.

*

My own first direct contact with Judaism was being taken to the Jewish Community Seder in Dunedin when I was about ten. There were lots of old people there and only one or two other children. The other children were boys and they seemed to know all about what was going on.

There was a meal of sorts, but strange – a bowl of salt water, a hard-boiled egg, a sprig of parsley and some matzos. I knew that word, 'matzos'. Mainly, people were reading and singing from a book which opened at the back. One page was Hebrew writing and on the opposite page the Hebrew was transliterated into English letters. I tried to imagine that I was in a foreign country, listening to the radio. One day, out of all those voices, I would understand something. I tried to match the syllables to the sounds I heard, but the sounds moved on so quickly and even when I found a sound or a pattern of sound I had no idea what it meant. I could only watch; sit when they sat, eat when they ate, try to turn a page when everyone else did and hope that I did nothing wrong. The room was cold. Only one or two people spoke to me.

At around this time I also remember going with my mother to meet a very nice man with an accent who worked in the D.I.C., which was a department store. He wore a tape measure around his neck as a doctor wears a stethoscope.

*

In my parents' bookshelf in the 1960s there was a book with a burning wheel on the cover which described Nazi war crimes. I don't ever remember opening it in those years, or being told not to open it. It was just there, in the non-fiction section, next to a guide to the identification of New Zealand native trees and plants.

This year I saw a second-hand copy of this book in the window of Quilter's Bookshop and I bought it. I opened it once. It is from the early 1950s. It gives a lot of information, complete with black and white pictures which I won't describe. It sticks to the facts.

*

At roughly the same time as my great-grandfather was applying for citizenship, New Zealand elected its first Labour government. This was a time of killing chains and men who built their own houses and all that milk-and-meat-and-suspicion-of-artifice-and-decoration-and-foreigners and Jews-who-were-already-here-not-wanting-to-stand-out. Still today, the small number of Jews in New Zealand, their relative 'invisibility' culturally and politically, and the low level of anti-Semitism in New Zealand, are often spoken about together as if each one causes the others.[75]

---

75 Ann Beaglehole and Hal Levine, *Far From the Promised Land: Being Jewish in New Zealand*, Wellington: Pacific Press Ltd, 1995, p. 2.

This exact logic meant immigration of Jewish refugees from Hitler before the war was seen by the government of the day and by some New Zealand Jews as a threat. The first Labour government had other concerns too about immigrant Jews from Europe, such as a fear of immigrants driving down wages and increasing unemployment so soon after the Depression, and of possible damage to the livelihoods of local doctors and dentists.

Between 1936 and 1938 the New Zealand government declined 1731 applications from refugees for entry to New Zealand and granted 727.[76] Some of the 727 died, went to other countries, changed address or were imprisoned before being able to make their way to New Zealand. It is not possible to know what happened to the 1731[77] people whose applications were declined.

These are some of the places the refugees settled: Auckland, Hamilton, Glen Afton near Huntly, Palmerston North, Christchurch, North Canterbury, Pahiatua, Dunedin, Waiouru, Nelson and Hanmer.

In Wellington they settled in Upper Hutt, Petone, Northland and Kelburn Parade. I notice the places are urban and rural

---

76 Francis Arthur Ponton, 'Immigration Restriction in New Zealand: A Study of Policy from 1908–1939', MA thesis, University of New Zealand (Victoria), 1946, p. 114.

77 Since writing these sentences I have been told that the official figures are 'very unreliable' and that perhaps 16,000 people applied to the High Commission in London. The difference between these figures is extraordinary.

and in both islands, although apparently Wellington was the most popular place for Jewish refugees to settle.

In addition to any other concerns about opening immigration to Jews, 'resistance to importing to New Zealand problems of the old world, such as anti-Semitism, . . . influenced the government'.[78]

In 1939 Walter Nash, a Labour politician, wrote to a Labour Party official:

> There is a major difficulty of absorbing these people in our cultural life without raising a feeling of antipathy to them.[79]

It would be fair to say that in the 1930s *no one* wanted Jews to stand out in New Zealand. In Ann Beaglehole and Hal Levine's book on Jewish life in New Zealand, one of their refugee informants puts it like this:

> They [the established New Zealand Jews] believe that the more you blend in with the landscape, the less they (non-Jews) will notice you.[80]

---

78 Ann Beaglehole, *A Small Price to Pay: The Refugees from Hitler in New Zealand 1936–1946*, Wellington: Allen & Unwin New Zealand Ltd and Historical Branch, Department of Internal Affairs, New Zealand, 1988, p. 22.

79 Walter Nash, Letter to Mrs J. Hall, Secretary, Hororata Branch of the New Zealand Labour Party, 21 March 1939, quoted in Beaglehole, *A Small Price to Pay*, p. 16.

80 Beaglehole and Levine, *Far From the Promised Land*, p. 64. These interviews, done in the early 1990s, asked ninety-three Jewish people, mostly former refugees, about their lives in New Zealand. I note the use of the present tense in this person's description of the New Zealand Jews' desire to blend in.

This is the New Zealand the pre-war and immediate post-war Jewish refugees came to. This is also the New Zealand of which my great-grandfather wanted, late in his life, to be a citizen.

*

According to a survey of anti-Semitism in New Zealand from the end of World War II until the early 1980s, quoted in Beaglehole and Levine, incidents of a 'malevolent' kind, such as the defacement of graves, occurred in a series of outbursts with quite long periods between series, and tended to follow 'public comment or media programmes which focused on Jews'.[81]

*

In a thesis written at Victoria University of Wellington in 1946, Francis Ponton adds a little more to the picture of how Wellington was looking at its Jews at that time:

> We all know the criticism which has been levelled at 'the Jews' and as I write (May 1946)[82] there are anti-Jewish slogans chalked up on many walls in Wellington. Admittedly these appear in hotels and public lavatories and may evidence little more than the activities of a fanatic with a cess-pool mind, but at the same time I feel that there is a definite feeling against the Jews in New Zealand.[83]

---

81 Ibid., p. 91.
82 Ponton's parenthetical note.
83 Ponton, 'Immigration Restriction in New Zealand', p. 107.

I am shocked. This is not a Wellington and a New Zealand I like to think of.

My sceptical friend asked me recently why I was so much more shocked at this description of anti-Jewish slogans on toilet walls than at the unsympathetic views of Walter Nash. It takes me some time to arrive at the answer and during this time I make a joke about the state of pub lavatories and another joke about the cynicism of politicians. Although I have read that media focus on Jews is associated with a rise in anti-Semitism, this immediate post-war anti-Jewish feeling among New Zealanders who must know at least something of the destruction of European Jewry, is the first example of this phenomenon that I have really seen. That is the real reason that I am shocked.

*

On 19 October 2012, the same day I read Mr Ponton's beautifully written and cool-headed thesis, I heard that Jewish graves had been defaced in Auckland.

*[84]

84 An asterisk is often a request for a certain period of silence, but this particular asterisk identifies a subject on which much more could be said.

Abe's stories

As a child, Daniel Mendelsohn, author of *The Lost: A Search for Six of the Six Million*, used to write to his grandfather Abe in Miami and ask questions about the names and dates of birth of his relations. Abe would help if he could, but sometimes he did not know the answers to Daniel's questions.

On his visits to the family in New York, Abe told Daniel stories, all of which proceeded in 'vast circling loops',[85] each story containing another, each event needing to be explained by another story and another, a method which Abe was happy to explain to Daniel; stories to be found buried inside each other like Russian dolls, he said, not sitting beside each other like dominoes.

Abe's stories are about everything, Daniel realises, except Abe's older brother Sam, Sam's wife and his four daughters, all *killed by the Nazis*, as family members used to say, whenever the subject came up. These six people were, from Daniel's point of view, 'not so much dead as lost, vanished from the world',[86] as well as from his grandfather's stories. This *absence* sends Daniel off on a decades-long search for information about what happened to these six people. The search itself is the subject of *The Lost*.

---

85 Daniel Mendelsohn, *The Lost: A Search for Six of the Six Million*, New York: Harper Collins Publishers, 2006, p. 32.

86 Ibid., p. 15.

At the end of his search, looking back on these childhood times, Daniel Mendelsohn finds that already, in his childhood, he had lots of important pieces of information about these six people, but somehow did not fully understand what he had. This is what he knew as a child:

> Sam and his wife and four beautiful daughters,
> one of whom was called Bronia, were *killed by*
> *the Nazis*,
>
> Sam had some trucks and the Nazis wanted trucks,
>
> Sam was one of the first on the list,
>
> They were hiding in a *kessle*,
>
> A neighbour turned them in,
>
> Their shiksa maid turned them in,
>
> They raped them and killed them all.

For a while, when he is young, Daniel thinks the place they hid is a 'castle', the word said by his grandfather in his particular accent. Daniel wonders if a kindly Polish aristocrat took in a Jewish butcher and his children.

But no, after circumnavigating the world and finally returning to a place he had been before, Daniel finds the *kessle*. It is a hole, dug eight or nine feet deep and three feet wide into the earth, under the floor of the living room in a house in Bolechow[87] in Ukraine; the house now occupied by alcoholics or drug addicts from southern Russia. Daniel forces himself to climb down into the hole and finds himself thinking of a coffin. *Kestl*, it turns out, means 'box' in Yiddish.

*

I find, as I write this list of what Daniel knew, that I had not, on the first, or second, or even third time of reading his book, really noticed the matter of Sam's trucks. More and more, in the last year, I have been noticing the role that the drive to accumulate wealth played in the Holocaust.

*

All the time he was telling stories to his grandson, Abraham's own story was still happening. Abraham Jaeger's story involved many languages, towns with several names and several wives as well as a brother lost in the Holocaust or perhaps abandoned along with his wife and four girls. Daniel's quest takes him everywhere and lasts many years. He labours endlessly, questioning old men and women and piecing together what might be true and what might not be true. He finds several guides. Luck plays a part too, but in

87 Bolechow was a village near Lemburg (now L'viv) 'in the province of Galicia in the Imperial and Royal Empire of the Dual Monarchy of Austro-Hungaria' (ibid., p. 65). The town is now called Bolekhiv. I use the old spelling 'Bolechow' when speaking of Mendelsohn's quest.

the end, it turns out that some of the most important information was right under his nose.

*

Daniel Mendelsohn is an energetic and thorough researcher. He makes use of family photographs and their captions. He reads old letters. He looks between the lines. As he goes along he meets a man in Israel who is keeper of all information about Bolechow's Jews.

This man tells Mendelsohn the names of people who might know something that could help him fill in his white space. When Daniel hears of old people who might know something about his great-uncle and his family he crosses the world to meet them. He interviews them carefully, keeping quiet about what he already knows so that they will tell him what they think is correct.

He asks them endless detailed questions. Sometimes these meetings involve eating enormous meals which elderly ladies have cooked, despite their failing health, because they knew he was coming to talk about the old country. He records all these interviews. He brings his brother, a photographer, along so that he will have a photographic record. That brother is willing to ask two elderly men to sit in a car for twenty minutes, roll up their trousers and walk into the sea at Bondi Beach, and then ask a surfer to walk backwards and forwards behind the two men because that would be the best photograph of Holocaust survivors in Australia.

'My job is playing bad cop to people until they reach the breaking point. I need a picture that says "Australia", otherwise why did I come?' he says.[88]

Sometimes, as I read Daniel Mendelsohn's book, I worried about these elderly people he was interviewing. I wondered who would help them with the dishes after he left and whether they would be able to sleep. Maybe they stayed drunk for three days after his visit, or had a heart attack? I wondered if he ever stopped before he had finished his enquiries, just because it would be considerate.

I thought that if it were me, I would rather miss something important than dig deep like a surgeon. I would rather lose a photographic edge than ask an old man to get his feet wet.

*

Mendelsohn thought at first that Bolechow existed only in frozen form in the remote past. But during his research he found that Bolechow was closer to him than he thought. There were still old people in Bolekhiv who had lived in the town when it was called Bolechow. Mendelsohn met these human bridges. People from Bolechow were present in America, pinching his cheek and staring at him, at family parties during his childhood. At that time he hid from them, finding them weird and scary.

88 Mendelsohn, *The Lost*, p. 257.

Sometimes, in the midst of his 512-page text, Mendelsohn inserts the word '*Listen*'. When I look at page 64, as an example, to see what follows the imperative, it is a description of how Mendelsohn's decision to use a Jewish genealogical website leads to a man contacting him which leads in turn to information about an elderly woman he had known as a child, a woman who used to touch his face and weep when she saw him. *Now*, with this new information, he understands who she was. This leads him to consider what she could have told him, if he had been old enough or interested enough to ask.

At the end of this exploration Mendelsohn finds his own guilt – guilt that he missed the opportunity to learn what these old people knew. This guilt tips him off the couch, away from the internet and onto the plane, to all the places where other old people from Bolechow now live. Bolechow is the Point Last Seen. The place to concentrate the search. Without the website, he would never have taken this action. Without being in Bolechow he would never have found the 'kessle'.

When Mendelsohn says 'Listen', I think he is telling us several things; that searching for what is lost is important, that once you have noticed the loss, the search should not be delayed and that a search is best done by diving into the deepest water and creating lots of noise and movement so that certain other people will be drawn to what you are doing. You don't know who they are. That is part of the point. You have to put yourself into a place where they will notice you.

The exact opposite of swimming with sharks.

This Crazy Thing a Life

As a direct result of all my reading, I make up ten rules to guide me in my own research.

1. I will not phone deaf old ladies out of the blue. I will arrange to be vouched for, and introduced.
2. I will not bang on people's front doors with my fist, or any metaphorical version of that.
3. I will try to recognise Yiddish words.
4. I will answer questions about my parents, my marital status, number of children, their degrees and their incomes, without flinching.
5. I will make sure I always have a clean hanky.
6. I will try to say German words correctly.
7. *Schpielberg* is the correct pronunciation of the name of the movie director.
8. I will not interrupt old people when they are telling me their story, except if there is a fire alarm.
9. I will not cry unless they do.
10. If they are women, they were beautiful when they were young.

*

After I find a book with the title *This Crazy Thing a Life*[89] I add Rule 11: *Life* is crazy. People are getting by.

---

89 Richard Freadman, *This Crazy Thing a Life: Australian Jewish Autobiography*, Crawley: University of Western Australia Press, 2007.

*

Much later, having noticed the contributions made by Billy Pilgrim, the Tralfamadorians, Jacques Austerlitz and a man called Bloomfield from the suburb of Carlton in Melbourne,[90] I add two more rules, these to be applied *ex post facto*.

12. It is important to find out things but even more important to avoid harming natural people.
13. Fictional people do not look you in the eye or feel pain. They are available without appointment, and at very little expense. Furthermore, their well-being is not of concern to any official bodies. They therefore make excellent research participants, and will be considered whenever possible as a preferable alternative to natural people or the natural descendants of dead people.

---

90 Bloomfield, trying to live his life after the war, appears on pages 230 and 265–6.

For an hour or two I am a witness for the witness

I met a total of six elderly men and women who go to museums and meet people like me, hoping that with their own bodies and voices, they will give the story of the Holocaust of European Jews the power of the real.

> If you did not:
> see
> hear
> smell
> feel
> taste
> Then:
> you were not there.[91]

They wonder if we really believe them that they lost almost everyone they knew. They find themselves still forced to speak, seventy-odd years later, for everyone – their young wives and serious boyfriends, the baby sister their parents doted on, their cheeky brothers, all the children in the school photograph and all the children never born. It is an act of persuasion which has, as all such acts do, an uncertain outcome. They do not expect miracles. They do not even expect courtesy.

They hope, by exhibiting themselves outside of any glass case, protected only by their skin and clothes, to reach us in

91 Liba, *The Holocaust – Between Me and Myself*, p. 21.

a way that no other sort of museum object could. They reach out towards us by allowing us to reach out towards them. It is an extraordinary act.

None of them says Jews should keep a suitcase packed. None of them speaks about the failure of the Enlightenment or loss of faith in German *Kultur*. They speak of what happened to *them* and sometimes this happens to contain one of the common experiences which have become the icons of these stories. It is this way round.

As individuals, they reach back to events so terrible that we can hardly believe someone could have lived through them, and forward, to the future, where young people live. They hope to change us into slightly different people from the ones we were before. They want us to be braver than we usually are and give more of ourselves to protecting whoever is being singled out today for cruel treatment. I know these things because when I was brave enough I asked what caused them to act in this way, and sometimes, when I didn't ask, I saw the answer later in the books they have written.

Excuse me Madam

In November 2011 I sat for an hour or more with a man who came to the museum on a certain day every week, to tell his story. As I walked through the museum I saw him talking with a middle-aged man, then I saw the middle-aged man walk away. I'm not quite sure what happened next but I remember thinking the old man looked very frail and saying perhaps we should sit down. He must have agreed because we sat down side by side on a padded bench seat and he started to tell me about how he survived.

This was the first time anyone ever looked straight at me and told me a story like this. I did not expect this situation to develop as quickly as it did and I did not stop him to ask if he would be willing to sign a consent form and to remind him that talking about the Holocaust might be upsetting for him.

At first I was his only audience. After some time two other women caught his eye. He stood up and walked towards them. 'Excuse me Madam, would you like to hear my story?' he asked. They joined us.

I noticed that his story proceeded in loops, coming back after lengthy movements to particular points. These points acted like the intersection of several important roads. From one of these crossroad points the story could go in several possible directions. This meant that if a new person arrived – something he strongly encouraged – he could carry on towards the nearest crossroad and then choose which road to go down for the new audience.

I also noticed certain concentrations of attention. The German man who shared news from the Eastern Front with him, and sometimes his sandwich, was one. The fact that the road he lifted stones for and the airport he carried wood for were never finished or used was another. His conscientious approach to work and the importance of staying out of trouble was another. The people he met and the things he did in the days just before and after he liberated himself were the last.

I suppose he would have many possible structures and concentrations, depending on who he was talking to. Bloomfield from Carlton, a fictional man who hardly ever spoke, used to visit a woman who had been on the same boat with him coming to Australia. A boat-sister, he called her. He would wait and watch until he thought all her family was out then slide along the hall and sit at her kitchen table. She would talk to him and no one else about voices and dybbuks which tormented her. He would intone the word 'Yes' in a strange sing-song voice, over and over again.

I saw other people there too, visitors to the museum like me. I saw that each of us asked our own questions. One woman, also from New Zealand, asked the man if he had a number tattooed on his arm. No. A girl of fourteen asked the man what he would say to Hitler if he met him now. They wouldn't let me near him, the tiny man in the tweed jacket said, and in that moment I saw him as dangerous. Did you ever see your parents again, asked a woman with her eleven-year-old daughter beside her. No.

It was four o'clock. Museums close at four o'clock. 'Tell all your friends to come here,' one of the men said to me as we walked out of the gallery.

*

Missing from this account: her warm hands, his hand on my shoulder, his hold on my arm, his blue eyes, her brown eyes, two brown suits, dyed hair, lipstick, gold jewellery, natty shoes, one walking stick, quite a lot of kisses, her tears, my tears, his trembling chin. A comment about Australia – of course there are instances of anti-Semitism here too, but only by a few individuals – not the government. And her eyes, which became black, turned away from us, and saw things which she kept to herself.

The facts

The notion of facts in relation to the Holocaust is very very important to people who survived it and to those who support them. They are afraid at the deepest possible level that the rest of us just will not believe that these things happened. Watching one day as a busload of burly fifteen-year-old Australians arrived at a museum with their teachers to hear about the Holocaust, seeing their powder-blue blazers and the way the boys bashed into each other on purpose and laughed when someone was knocked off his feet, I wondered if they had it in them to hear about this.

I wondered if they would see the tiny white-haired man speaking to them in heavily accented English as an object of ridicule. But I had underestimated both the white-haired man and the fifteen-year-old Australians. For a few minutes, as the white-haired man in the very smart brown suit spoke about the complexity of political life in Poland in the 1930s it looked touch and go. But quite soon he started to tell them about his life in the Lodz ghetto and the job his father gave him – to build a hiding place for himself and his mother.

I could feel the atmosphere changing as he spoke about this. He told the students that one day his mother could no longer climb up into the hiding place. She said she intended to take a place on the transports. He told the students that he went with her to Auschwitz, hoping that he would be able to look after her a little.

*

At this point there was silence in the room. In the silence I looked around and noticed that the students were from many cultures. Who knows what stories of parting and love they had? A teacher sitting near me was crying.

*

Later the old man spoke about something he did which he was clearly proud of. He and a friend collected official posters listing all the restrictions on Jews and ordering the Jewish population of Lodz into the ghetto, and they packed them into a box, which they hid in the ghetto in the safest place they could think of – under a stinking toilet. Looking ahead, even in these circumstances, to a future after the war, he and his friend were desperate to have proof of what happened.

He went back, after the war, and found the box of posters. They hang on the wall of the museum, but after the talk, when the students went to look around the museum, I did not see the students looking at them.

I noticed that some of the boys stopped and looked at a model of Treblinka. This model was the most frightening object I saw in any of the museums. It occupied a space about the size of two dining tables and was enclosed in glass. I can't say exactly why it was so frightening. My first thought was that I was imagining the dreams and waking life of the man who made the model, a man with all this inside him.

The man who made this model was a carpenter after the war. Faced with the problem of finding suitable materials to make

Treblinka, he sometimes used dolls to represent people. Sometimes he used tiny soldiers. For the real branches of trees woven into the inner fence of the camp, he used the green plastic fringe that butchers use in their display windows to separate cuts of meat.

Later, when I thought more about the model itself, it seemed as though the particular green that he had painted all the watchtowers, the pile of little pink cloth corpses and the tiny leather whips which the guards held and trailed behind them, contained and emitted fear, as you would expect, and something else. Something inert. I found myself thinking about the word 'evil', an idea which I have always tried not to believe in.[92] My sceptical friend reads a draft of this text as I am writing. What do you mean? she says when she reads this page. Do you believe in evil or not? I tell her that I believe it is best to act as though evil does not exist, even if it does. This is when she tells me that she finds New Zealanders dangerously naïve.

I notice that Thomas Keneally also finds himself trying to decide if what happened in places like Plaszów was 'evil'. He decides that the SS men who guarded the camp were not themselves evil but were persuaded by distorted language to go further and further away from what they

92 I note that Hephzibah, a Jewish woman in *The Finkler Question* by Howard Jacobson, attempts to keep the word anti-Semitism out of her mind. It was, she believed, something you keep locked away. One day it forces itself into her vision in the form of bacon rashers wrapped around the door handles of her Museum of Anglo-Jewish Culture.

knew was right until they ended up doing evil. I want to believe this, but I find the concentration on language distortions a bit too simple.

Perhaps I should just focus on what is in front of me? The model of Treblinka evokes feelings. Whatever they are called, I should let them be inside me.

This model has entered the vortex of controversy surrounding every depiction of the Holocaust. Some say that if it is described as a model, it must be factually accurate in every respect. If it was wrong in some detail, they say, a chink would open into which doubt could be inserted. If the model is wrong, perhaps the museum cannot be trusted? If the museum cannot be trusted, perhaps the Holocaust cannot be trusted? It is safer to describe it as a 'conceptual model', a mind map, or an artwork.

The day before I saw the conceptual model of Treblinka, and in a different museum, I was reading small cards of text. I have heard that curators in some museums have begun to identify themselves and describe their curatorial processes, in a bid to give visitors a more complete picture of how an exhibit comes to look the way it does. The idea that a curtain might be pulled back on the curatorial process is of great interest to me. I saw no signs of it in any museums I visited. I heard about committees to advise curators and serious research into objects and their contexts. I also heard that an exhibition is the voice of the museum, not the voice of particular individuals.

The museum has removed some pieces from the conceptual model of Treblinka and changed others. In one place small pink plastic dolls have been replaced by plaster-of-Paris figures and a baby impaled on a pitchfork has been removed. The reason for this, according to Inga Clendinnen, is that the dolls and the spitted baby might make visiting schoolboys laugh.[93] Soldier figures have been removed, because there were no soldiers at Treblinka. Miniature floodlights have been removed and the model has been enclosed in glass.

I had always imagined that a particular object would either be included in or omitted from a museum's exhibition. It interests me that curating reaches right inside this object and changes it to fit the voice of the museum. But then I think of editors who might ask for a certain paragraph to be removed and I think that editors and curators take part in the act of bringing these expressions into the public gaze, this action paid for with the surrender of certain rights over the material.

---

93 Inga Clendinnen, 'Building Treblinka', *Agamemnon's Kiss: Selected Essays*, Melbourne: The Text Publishing Company, 2006, p. 169.

The hole

At about the time I was writing about the Holocaust survivors I met in the museums and the guards at Auschwitz, I found the sculpture *Rudderstone*[94] in the Botanic Gardens in Wellington. The sculpture has two faces. The one facing the path shows the Old World as shiny black mica-flecked granite. The black granite is also said to represent the night sky. There is a curved hole in the black granite, which a sign encourages viewers to walk through. According to this sign, if I accept that challenge and walk through that hole, I take my body on a physical and metaphorical journey from old to new.

This is exactly it, I thought. The Old World is where the Holocaust happened. In Poland most of all. The sky over there is black. Heavy and thick with ash. The people over there hated Jews so much that they killed nearly all of them and probably nothing much has changed. That place over there is the Old World. ('Over there' is a term preferred by Israelis, I am told, but making good sense from here too.)

I took some photographs of the black side of the sculpture. I also looked through the hole to see what would be waiting for me if I went through to the New World. It was like looking through a keyhole. I saw a short path leading towards a stand of bush. I took a photograph of this too.

---

94 Denis O'Connor, *Rudderstone*, 1997, Botanic Garden, Wellington.

Then I walked through the hole and found myself on the other side, looking at white and blue marble. According to the sign, white is the sky and blue is the sea; the blue in the mind's eye of everyone who lives on the Pacific. I let my eyes linger on that blue. I belong to that blue and it belongs to me.

I let my eyes sweep across all the swirls and shades of the blue. There are some small, irregularly shaped pieces of black in there. I am fine with the fact that there are small clumps of black in the swirls of blue. They are pieces of the Old World that came with us. And, human nature being what it is, there might have been blackness here already. But mostly we have blue here. That is the point.

I look through the hole from the blue side, back towards the black side. I am astonished to see that a short path leads to a stand of bush. The bush there is the same perfect green as the bush on the blue side. The trees are as tall, perhaps taller. In the light of this finding I look further at the irregularly shaped clumps of black in the blue swirls. There are more of them than I first thought, and some of them have a brown area around the black which seems as though it is on its way to turning black.

Yes, said one reader. Fair enough. We have black here, but it is only brownish black. Not really *black* black.

The Holocaust Gallery at the Auckland War Memorial Museum

I see from the floor plan that the Holocaust Gallery is small. It surprises me that it has no door. You walk into it, if you decide to do that, from a white balcony beneath a grand stained-glass window. Around the walls of the balcony the names of New Zealand soldiers who died in World War I are carved in stone. Light falls on their names.

The inscription beside the names of these men reads:

> They whom inscription upon these walls commemorate are those who at the call of King and country left all that was dear to them, endured hardness and finally passed out of the sight of men by the path of duty and self-sacrifice, giving their lives that others may live in freedom. Let those who come after see to it that their names not be forgotten.

The Holocaust Gallery has a plaque which reads:

> Auckland War Memorial Museum gratefully acknowledges the support it has received in the preparation of this exhibit from the Auckland Jewish Community and the New Zealand Lottery Grants Board.

*

My friend from the museum industry says it matters what you see when you go into or come out of a museum. When he said this I thought immediately of a book. The front cover, the title, the bibliography – all the things that start shaping your expectations and responses before you even notice that it is happening. Sometimes you don't understand these references until after you have the book inside you.

My friend spoke of his visit to Yad Vashem, in Jerusalem. The land in Israel is harsh, he said, and the light is harsh too, so when you step out of the museum you are in bright light and you are in a place which you know is almost unbelievably old. Judged by the language of signposts and the names on buses, you are in a Jewish world, but you know that everyone has been here and you know that this is the most fought-over city in the world.

Compare that with coming out of the Holocaust Museum in Washington D.C., he said. The United States Holocaust Memorial Museum is located in American Museum headquarters. Within a short distance are the National World War II Memorial, the Korean War Veterans Memorial, the Vietnam Veterans Memorial, the National Museum of the American Indian, the National Air and Space Museum, the German American Friendship Garden and many more.

You soon get the idea, he said. The Holocaust of the Jews is a significant event for America, but only one of many.

Thinking about the expectations set up by the Holocaust Gallery in its context in the Auckland War Memorial Museum, I would have to conclude that the Holocaust was an aspect of war, that it was small and contained and much less significant in New Zealand than World War I or II and that its depiction in this place relies on energy and money from the Jewish community and charity.

*

The Holocaust Gallery really *is* a small room. It is dark in there and opera music plays softly in the background. This music is not grand, or beautiful or comforting. It affects me in the same way as a single high note from a violin played over and over. The day of my visit, one middle-aged man, one young Asian woman and her two small children were in there. When I walked in, the man left. I paced out the room and found that it is approximately 8 metres long and 3.5 metres wide.

On the walls there are glass cases containing photographs and small pieces of text. There are two telephones mounted on the wall and two wooden stools. At the time of my visit one of the children, aged perhaps three or four, had one of the telephones up to his ear. At first he just stood there then something he heard made him laugh and he handed the telephone to his mother. She hung up.

I looked more closely at these telephones and found that there was a menu of thirty-two stories which you could hear if you pressed a numbered button, a bit like a jukebox except that only you would hear the story. Later I was very struck by the fact that these telephones only worked in one direction.

*

‘Press a button to listen to a personal story’ says a notice. If the sun is shining outside, and it often is in Auckland, you might begin in a hopeful way with #27, Hidden by Righteous Gentiles – the one about a man who said to his Jewish friend ‘Come to me if you are ever in trouble’ and meant it – you hear his name – he is dead now – and no, he didn’t do it for the money, although a certain amount of money did change hands.

*

You might sit on one of two round wooden stools attached to the wall an awkward distance from the telephones, and you might listen to #27, which had a happy ending, and after that you might try one about someone hiding under the stairs when the Gestapo came, and you might think that this person must have survived to tell this story, but that is only two stories and there are thirty-two.

So – sooner or later you always end up with #31, The Guards at Auschwitz, which, in the shadows of this small room, I misread as The *Sparks* at Auschwitz, no doubt due in part at least to *Fire, Fireflies, Fire roses, Kristall, a burning night, stars, the chamber of smoke, smoke without a shape*, signals and signs of the poet Rose Ausländer, whose work I was reading just before my visit to the museum.

This week, as I write about the Holocaust Gallery, I am also reading Jorge Semprún's description of his first few months after being released from Buchenwald.[95] At night, in Paris, lying beside a beautiful young woman to whom he has made love, he is woken by a memory of the guards shouting over the loudspeaker. *Crematorium ausmachen*! they scream. Crematorium shut down! They say this because flames rising from the chimney might attract Allied night bombers.

*

My friend who works in the museum industry said that not all visitors to museums are seeking the same thing. He himself is seeking a moment of connection. A 'transformational moment', he called it. I had two moments of connection in the Holocaust Gallery of the Auckland War Memorial Museum. The first was when I saw the story of a small wooden urn, which sat on a shelf in one of the glass cases. I was grateful for the inscription beside the urn. By itself the urn would have said 'ashes' to me but nothing more.

The story on the card says that Karel Beran, an Auschwitz survivor, went back to the camp on 16 September 1946 and, witnessed by 'a senior government official', one Dr Armin Glanz, took ashes from the crematorium. These ashes came to New Zealand with Mr Beran. For some years he kept the ashes from Auschwitz in this wooden urn. I picture it on

---

95 Jorge Semprún, *Literature or Life*, trans. Linda Coverdale, New York: Penguin Books, 1997.

the top shelf of his wardrobe, next to his hats. The ashes are buried now, the card says.

*

If Semprún is to be believed, in the first few days after Buchenwald was 'liberated', he and some of the other survivors at the camp were talking about how they would try to convey 'what happened' to people who had not been there. The group was a sort of Who's Who of French and European literature and philosophy, lifted from the streets and salons of Paris and taken, via other camps, to Buchenwald. They used to meet, while each person could, on Sunday afternoons, to celebrate all things French. Often they were physically unrecognisable to each other but instead recognised each other by quotations and ideas.

Their discussion that day in April 1945, which Semprún described in the 1990s, foreshadowed and summarised a thousand similar discussions about how to convey what really happened in the Holocaust and what the Holocaust really meant.

I think of this discussion as another sort of set piece. Semprún sets the arguments out for philosophical and artistic scrutiny.

Some of the survivors think that conveying what happened to people who were not there could best be done by sticking to the facts. Some, like Semprún, think it could best be done by the use of just enough art to make it possible for people to understand what was being described. Perhaps there will be a 'Literature of the camps', he suggests, rather disingenuously.

They are sure of one thing, these men in Buchenwald, that all the work of scholars, the compilation of documents and eye-witness accounts will miss the essential truth of their experience.

A professor turns to Semprún and smiles. The artifice of a work of art, he says, is their best hope.

Semprún's own view wins. Art, but not too much, will be needed to describe the camps. But after all this laying out of positions, another problem is raised. No matter how they are told, their stories will not be easily believable. This time no solution is found. There are questions too about those who will be listening to these stories of the camps. How hard will they try to understand what they are being told?

*

One evening the young Semprún, living through his first summer as a survivor, and his girlfriend, enter an apartment where all the furniture is covered by white sheets. Semprún is overwhelmed by unease brought on by the white sheets, and does not know why. His unease grows and grows and he feels he will die, or that he *must* die. Semprún leaves the beautiful woman's bed, walks the streets of Paris until dawn when he knocks on the door of a woman he knows who is a writer. She will neither make him talk nor stop him talking. This makes her a refuge.

*

I connect Karel Beran and Jorge Semprún, both trying to be alive after their release. I wonder if Karel Beran had someone he could visit at dawn or whenever he felt most oppressed.

I try to imagine a former prisoner making the decision to return to Auschwitz. I try to imagine this man making his feet take him onto a train going to Auschwitz.

I imagine a mixture of chaos and red tape and officials who might have been part of the Nazi administration.

I wonder why he went this particular day.

Is it coincidence that the first Nuremberg trials were just about to end, or that in 1946, 16 September fell during the month of preparations for the High Holy Days? I wonder if the purpose of the trip was to bring ashes away or whether that act was something he felt moved to do on the spot, when he was there?

I imagine this man finding a tool or making his hands into a tool to scrape ashes from an oven into some container. I do not have him beside me to tell me why or how he was able to do this. But even from my sunny room on this windy spring day, more than sixty years later, I know this was an important act.

*

The second moment of transformation for me in the Holocaust Gallery was seeing a letter, written in 1938, by a man who worked for the Department of Customs.

Late in that year, when he was probably already thinking of the pleasure of cricket down at the Basin over Christmas, or of yarning the afternoon away over a couple of warm flagons, he wrote, on behalf of the Minister of Customs, to a man on the other side of the world.

No, he said. The government of New Zealand had declined the application for a permit to enter New Zealand. He added the following paragraph to his letter.

> It is considered therefore that it would be hardly worth your while making further application for a permit to enter New Zealand, it has recently been found necessary to discontinue the issuing of such permits except in very special circumstances.[96]

I have written letters for other, more senior, people too. I am familiar with the general muddiness and confusion of things people say and do and the tiny pleasure to be found in a set of circumstances fitting any criterion at all. I also admit to a pleasant sense of order and a slightly aggressive satisfaction from constructing a well-written 'No'.

---

96 Ann Beaglehole, 'The Response of the New Zealand Government to Jewish Refugees and Holocaust Survivors, 1933–1947', *Holocaustcentre.org.nz*, accessed 12 October 2012.

But what would the definition of 'very special circumstances' have been in December 1938? As I have said before, there was no quota to fill, and there were no set criteria for processing applications for entry to New Zealand at this time. Each application was considered individually.

Clearly the decision had nothing to do with fear, or hunger, or cold, or lack of legal rights, or soft-boned children, or trains, or dogs or guns, or isolation or desperation. In fact, referring to any of these probably counted against someone.

Three ingredients of success come up often in discussions of applications from European Jews for permits to enter New Zealand before the War.

Contacts Money and Luck.[97]

In my mind this man who worked at the Department of Customs was entirely satisfied with his letter, which slammed shut the door to New Zealand for one particular Jewish family from Europe, in 1938. I mentally convicted him of anti-Semitism, even if I never said that word. But when I told this story to someone else who also works for the government, she said she wondered if later he looked back on his letter and felt guilty. Her question seemed to open the door to viewing this man with more compassion.

*

97 Beaglehole, *A Small Price to Pay*, p. 14.

I would have liked to read some files of correspondence between the Customs Department and applicants for entry to New Zealand, to see exactly which circumstances matched which response, but a fire in 1952 destroyed Customs files from this period.

*

When I came home and thought about this small dark room in the Auckland War Memorial Museum, I thought I would like to write about the experience of visiting this room in a poem. The poem would be in the shape of a brick, like the room. I sat down at the table and tried to make a poem in the shape of a brick. But my poem would not make a brick. Instead it made an awkward thing – lumps, linked by joints, like the carriages of a train. My poem focused on the rigid stools and the one-way telephones. It was burdened by too many connections. I threw it away.

*

Lodz is a place in Poland, which is supposed to be pronounced something like *Lodge* or *Wooj*. Once, when I was speaking to a staff member about my reasons for visiting a Holocaust museum, I said the word 'loss'. The museum staff member thought I said 'Lodz'. When he is at work, and perhaps even more at home, he brings a list of ghettos and camps to the table.

*

I have already mentioned the occasion when I thought some words said 'the sparks at Auschwitz' when they really said 'the guards at Auschwitz' and my theory that this could be explained by the fact that in July and August 2011 I tried to translate some poems by Rose Ausländer.

There were perhaps fifteen of us who worked on making English translations of some of her poems. As each person spoke I could hear the same four elements in different proportions: love for the German language, a feeling for poetry, interest in the Holocaust and a connection with Europe. One man, who may have had all the other elements too, said nostalgia for the Austro-Hungarian Empire drew him to Ausländer and the poets of Czernowitz.

I found myself first allowing and then encouraging a sort of parallel chattering as I read Ausländer's algebraic poems until, by the end, every novel I ever read about what happened to Jewish people during the war was present and every personal account I had ever heard of how they felt and how they tried to live afterwards was speaking in my mind. This was what I brought to the table to meet her poems.

I heard a recording of Ausländer reading some of her poems. She had an unusually deep voice for a woman. This voice of unassailable authority, the tight rhythms of her German and her sparks made me feel like a schoolgirl.

A cake and a budgie

'You can't expect New Zealand people, who never even had to lock their doors at night, to understand such terrible things, but still they tried to understand.'[98] A woman called Herta Hochberg said this to Ann Beaglehole on 19 March 1987.

Herta had been in various camps, including Auschwitz and Bergen-Belsen, for four years before coming to New Zealand after the war. Her first job was as a machinist in a sewing factory. On the day of her birthday the girls gave her a big party with a cake and a budgie for a present.

> They knew, these ordinary New Zealand girls, what I had been through. They didn't understand it of course. They thought: 'She has been through a lot.'[99]

The number of Holocaust survivors who were permitted to settle in New Zealand after the war is uncertain but Beaglehole uses a figure of 300 survivors between 1945 and 1948 as a possible generous estimate.[100] Official policy remained the same as before the war. There were no set criteria for admission of refugees. Nor was preference given to close relatives of those refugees who had settled in New Zealand before the war.

---

98 Ibid., p. 48.
99 Ibid.
100 Beaglehole, *A Small Price to Pay*, p. 122.

Between 1948 and 1952 a total of 4500 displaced people came to New Zealand. These included some Jewish refugees, despite 'policy which still stressed that Jews and Slavs should be excluded'.[101]

*

The refugees' attitude to the German language and to German culture was 'mixed'.[102] On one hand pleasure in the German language had been killed by its association with orders and cruelty. George Steiner said later that after the Nazis, the German language 'made noise but created no sense of communion'.[103] On the other hand German was the language of much-loved books and poems. Some refugees tried to forget that German was their language. Some spoke it at home so that their children would be bilingual. Some didn't want their children to speak it. Some came back to it in old age.

Apparently one man threw out all his German books but read German newspapers. There is also a story about the Swiss Consul's dog, called by his English name 'Joe' in the street, but his German name 'Sett' at home.[104]

---

101 Ibid., p. 6.
102 Ibid., p. 57.
103 George Steiner, 'The Hollow Miracle', *Language and Silence: Essays 1958–1966*, London: Faber and Faber, 1967, p. 117.
104 Beaglehole, *A Small Price to Pay*, p. 58.

Do come to the City Hotel

A man called Salomon Holzer, writing under the pen name Ben Akiba, published a novel in Wellington in 1944 called *Who Sow in Tears.*[105] This novel provides a rare glimpse from that time of what the refugees thought of *us*. The main character is Mr Rosen, a man from Czechoslovakia who owns a factory in Sydney where he manufactures woollen rugs. His wife and children were all left behind in Europe and the book is much concerned with Mr Rosen's loneliness and desire for a certain refugee woman whose neck is graceful like his wife's and whose eyebrows are dark like a Jewish boy scholar's.

Holzer lived in Wellington, not Sydney, at the time he wrote the book, and Steven Sedley believes 'Sydney' should be read as a substitution for Wellington.[106] It is clear that Holzer was concerned about writing a book about this sort of situation while living in a very small community within a very small country. 'The characters in this book are the invention of the author who takes his ideas from human nature,' he says in the front of the book. 'Any similarity of names or places is entirely accidental and merely a coincidence. Any person attempting to bestow on himself any of

105 Ben Akiba [Salomon Holzer], *Who Sow in Tears*, Wellington: Eshape Publishing Co., 1944.

106 Steven Sedley, 'Reflecting on the World: Jewish Writers', *Jewish Lives in New Zealand*, ed. Leonard Bell and Diana Morrow, Auckland: Random House New Zealand, 2012, p. 119. (According to Sedley, Eshape Publishers, which Akiba says has its headquarters at P.O. Box 5036, Wellington C1, did not exist.)

the characteristics or personalities in this book will be considered as a trespasser.'

The story itself moves by personal narrative and anecdotes. In a few of these the author opens a shutter, shows a New Zealand scene, and closes it again, returning to the larger theme of Mr Rosen's torturous desire and his examination of Jewish wisdom for how it might assist him.

*

A German general and an English general, together in a room on the first floor of a building, compare their fighting men. They each have one soldier. One after the other, each general orders his soldier to march across a room and out an open window twenty feet above a stone courtyard. The German soldier obeys and breaks his leg. The English general's soldier is 'a volunteer from one of the Dominions, New Zealand'.[107] This man stops at the window, apologises politely to the general, and refuses to march out the window, explaining that he would injure himself if he obeyed. As Holzer describes this situation, he pauses after the word New Zealand, and inserts this sentence:

> The blue of the Tasman sparked in his eyes and the tan of the southern sun was still on his keen face.[108]

---

107 Akiba, *Who Sow in Tears*, p. 144.
108 Ibid.

This seems to be an explanation of some sort for the soldier's approach. Then Holzer carries on with the rest of the story, the order and the polite mutiny.

*

On a tram in Courtenay Place, Mr Rosen is rather reluctantly speaking German to a New Zealand Jew who wants to practise his German. A soldier home on leave hears them. When Mr Rosen and the soldier both get off the tram, the soldier challenges Mr Rosen.

'A foreigner eh? And how do you like our country? More than well? Happy here?'

'Yes, I am a foreigner,' Mr Rosen answers, 'I am from Czechoslovakia. I like this country and I would be happy here if the better part of myself did not remain in Europe.'

'What do you mean?' the soldier asks.

'I am sorry to say that my wife and four children are still there. Only I escaped. I left first as my life was in more direct danger.'

'Sorry,' the soldier says. He takes Mr Rosen's arm. 'Do come to the City Hotel and have a spot. We must become friends.'

Mr Rosen declines. 'Thank you very much,' he says, 'but I don't drink much.'[109]

*

In another, rather stranger exploration of New Zealand, Mr Rosen ponders the link between circumcision, which was favoured by the Plunket system and therefore much practised in New Zealand at that time, and the fact that 'the average New Zealander is just a little kindlier and more gentle than people I have met elsewhere'.[110]

---

109 Ibid., p. 145. Revisiting this conversation much later I find that after this rather testy exchange, Mr Rosen says, 'We parted friends'. I can imagine other interpretations.

110 Akiba, *Who Sow in Tears*, p. 143.

I ring the bell anyway

I had known for a few years that there was a Holocaust Centre in Wellington. At the time of my first visit, in March 2012, the Wellington Holocaust Research and Education Centre was about to be relaunched as the Holocaust Centre of New Zealand. From its beginning in 2006 it had been housed in a room which opens off Myers Hall, inside the Community Centre which is itself inside the Wellington Hebrew Congregation's building in Webb Street. On the street there is a flag inviting visitors to visit the Holocaust Centre, but, for security reasons, the door of the building is locked. Visitors are asked to ring a bell.

As a child of one of what Beaglehole and Levine call 'marginal and intermarried couples'[111] only fifty per cent of me feels confident of a welcome in this place, but I ring the bell anyway. Inside I am warmly welcomed and invited to look around and ask questions. I look around. I notice that there are display cases telling the story of two of the survivors who came to Wellington. Their stories are told in four parts: 'Before', 'The Lead Up', 'What Happened' and then 'Their lives in New Zealand'. There are photographs of a particular day in 1985 when one of these women told her story in public for the first time. I meet a woman who was there that day, in the audience. I am glad that this first telling of the story to the public of Wellington is part of the place that tells the story of the Holocaust.

---

111 Beaglehole and Levine, *Far From the Promised Land*, p. 54.

Hanging from a coat-hanger in its own glass case there is a dress given to a girl as she entered Auschwitz. It is made of heavy greyish fabric that looks like canvas. It has narrow shoulders and looks like a long shirt. I imagine this girl grown up, packing the dress into her suitcase when she came here. I imagine it folded, next to her sponge bag and her winter jerseys.

I talk about my interest in the Holocaust. I feel guilty because I haven't been to this place before but no one asks me why or makes me feel awkward.

I ask if anyone there knows the story of a small wooden urn I had seen at the Auckland War Memorial Museum's Holocaust Gallery and wanted to know more about. The card beside the urn said that the urn had contained ashes from Auschwitz which were brought to New Zealand by a man called Karel Beran.

I am given a name. I am told that this person has made oral history interviews with Holocaust survivors and might know the story of the man and the ashes and the urn. I email her. She answers me the same day. She has known Karel Beran all her life. 'Karel did an interview with the Shoah Foundation and I think you will find it in the collection at the Alexander Turnbull Library if you would like to listen to him in person,' she says.[112]

---

112 Claire Bruell, email to the author, 7 March 2012.

On my second visit to the Holocaust Centre, when the subject of family comes up, one of the volunteers asks me if I have seen the Honours Board listing the names of all the members of the Wellington Hebrew Congregation who served in World War I or II. My grandfather's name is there, together with his two brothers, Ernest and Bertie. Bertie has a gold Star of David beside his name, indicating that he 'made the ultimate sacrifice'.

I come away from the Holocaust Centre with a list of books about the Holocaust written by survivors who lived or live in the Wellington area. In one of those books I see photographs of a family living in Palmerston North. They lived there in the 1980s and 90s, as I did. They had holidays at Lake Taupo, as we did. Their house was in a pleasant leafy street where one of my friends now lives. I go home and think about the space between the point of my nose and my chest which seems to house as many objects as a magician's hat. I wonder what I am missing today.

*

The relaunch involves moving to a bigger space with new display cases and space for researchers to work. The relaunch attracts a big crowd including local and national politicians and members of the Diplomatic Corps. The German Ambassador is here. I speak with a Jewish man who 'comes from' several countries in Europe. He tells me with some intensity, in English, that the German Ambassador '*must*' be here. I nod. I think I know what the man means, but perhaps he is not convinced because he says it a different way and then another different way. 'The ambassador does not *choose* to be here', he says, and then 'he does not *want* to be here'.

I think about the German Ambassador, who might rather be at home, talking to his grandchildren by Skype, but *is* here, with hundreds of Jews, in Wellington, New Zealand, remembering the Holocaust *again*.

Yesterday I was talking with my friend in the museum industry about the relaunch. He is not Jewish. He told me that he had not known there was a Holocaust Centre in Wellington.

How, exactly, will that happen?

It has become a cliché for people to say that one reason for remembering the Holocaust is 'so that it won't happen again'. I always want to ask *how*, *exactly*, the act of remembering what happened, or passing that knowledge on, will stop it happening again. At the United Nations Holocaust Remembrance Day in 2011, three of the speakers described how they thought the mechanism might work.

One man, a politician, said that we should all step in to stop any extremist ideas from becoming established. Once established, extremist ideas develop their own momentum and become almost impossible to stop, he said.

Another man, a Māori leader, came up to the microphone in a puff of wind from the pine trees. He was at school here in Wellington with a man whose family came to New Zealand from Germany. That man was also at the ceremony. We didn't think of this when we were young, the Māori man said. He said that what he remembers best about the past is what the old people told him when he was a boy. Stories, he called them. Young people aren't going to read all this in books, he said. They might learn some things from a movie. But the best way to pass on to them *what happened*, is stories, stories, stories.

The last man to speak, a Jewish leader, began by saying how grateful Wellington's Jews are for the council's action in repairing damage done to Jewish headstones in 2004. We should all take away from this day the idea that the world is an imperfect place, he said. Our job is to try to improve the world around us – even if this is improvement is in small ways.

I have been thinking about the place of writing and of books in all this. A book could, perhaps without the writer's intention, contain old pieces of extremist ideas, broken down into tiny grains, worn smooth from all the times they have been handled. These grains could emit a high-pitched whistle, which members of a particular group hear and experience as very unpleasant, but most people, perhaps including the author, do not hear. My book might be whistling right now at a frequency I do not hear.

Warning

On my return from Australia, my sceptical polyglot friend asks me gently whether my visit was satisfying. I think for a while. I say yes. She asks me what exactly I saw there. I tell her that I met six people who had survived the Holocaust, and that I had not met any survivors before. She looks at me for a moment without speaking.

I tell her that they all said, in one way or another, that I could ask them questions. One man said 'you can ask me *any* questions'. I tell her that although it goes against my upbringing to ask my own burning questions of frail-looking, elderly men and women, I did.

Why do you do this? I asked one man, and the man said 'To warn everyone'. That part of his answer has a different quality from the rest of what he says. It is very direct. His voice is in a low register.

I heard the word 'warning' again in a speech at the United Nations Holocaust Remembrance Day ceremony here in Wellington. I think the speaker, a politician who was representing the City of Wellington, meant that the day and the ceremony were a warning because they made us remember the catastrophe. I assume the logic is that in the moment that we remember *what happened*, we are forced by that action to remember that these things *can* happen and therefore that they might start any day or have started already.

In a welcome moment of plain beauty, my notes of this Remembrance Day ceremony have the word 'warning' by itself on a line and underneath it, on the next line, the word 'bellbirds'.

'What do you think Australia should do about the boatloads of illegal immigrants arriving every week?' I asked the man in the museum, this question definitely not part of my plan but suddenly out of me. The man looks no more surprised by this question than by any other. He says it is a difficult matter. He has great sympathy for the people on the boats, coming with their families and risking their lives. His eyes water as he says this. But the state has to do what it needs to, he says. If the government did nothing, millions of immigrants would come from Asia. The government should do what is necessary, he says, but they shouldn't be cruel. That is the important thing.

*

The setting sun

I miss my childhood, an old man I met said, but I do not miss Poland.

His childhood // in Poland.

He pulls these carriages apart.

Something in his voice makes me wonder if they can really be un-hooked.

*

Bloomfield, who is never given a first name, looks back from Carlton in 1958 to Poland in the time 'before'. He remembers a season called 'Golden autumn':

> . . . the time of haybales and tired farmers making their way back home. The thatch upon village cottages trapped the setting sun within its folds. On the rooftops stood *bociany*, storks, erect in their massive nests. *Bociany* is Bloomfield's most loved Polish word. And storks perched upon thatched cottages, on guard, beside their nests, remains his most loved image of the time before.[113]

Bloomfield had two daughters in his nest. They were sent to the left, he to the right. One day in 1958 he sees leaves blown

113 Arnold Zable, *Scraps of Heaven*, Melbourne: Text Publishing, 2004, p. 81.

against a wire fence as a man impaled on an electric fence. Bloomfield falls to the ground, sensing guns pointed at him by the guards high above him in their watchtowers. As the Melbourne sun finally sinks Bloomfield sees only leaves again and wonders if storks are on their way.

A particular kind of conversation

I found the 318-minute video recording of Karel Beran being interviewed by Jason Walker in the audio-visual collection of the Victoria University Library during a search of the catalogue using the key words 'Holocaust' and 'New Zealand'. The catalogue entry looks like this:

> [Testimonies] [video recording] Survivors of the Shoah Visual History Foundation, pub. Shoah Foundation, 2005, L.A. Calif.

After that there is a long list of names, which have a number beside them, and no other explanation. If I had not visited the Wellington Holocaust Research and Education Centre and been given the name of a woman who had interviewed many Holocaust survivors in Auckland, and if she had not replied warmly to my email about Karel Beran and the story of the urn and told me that he had made an interview for the Survivors of the Shoah Visual History Foundation, I would never have realised what the catalogue entry meant – that if I searched through the fifty or sixty names, I would find Karel Beran's name.

The two DVDs of Karel Beran's interviews and all the other Shoah Foundation interviews from New Zealand are held in the Closed Reserve section of the library. No special permissions are required to watch these interviews. On my visit to the library to start watching the interviews I saw this inscription on the wall of a cubicle in the ladies' toilets:

> The holocaust is the shittiest thing to discuss.

I assumed that another student, with different interests from mine, had been required to find out more about the Holocaust than she wanted to. When I told a friend about this statement, she said she pictured a young woman in a tutorial, finding herself unable to think of anything she could safely say.

*

The purpose of the Shoah Foundation is:

> To overcome prejudice, intolerance and bigotry – and the suffering they cause – through the educational use of the Foundation's visual history testimonies.[114]

The interview with Karel Beran took place in Auckland on 10 December 1997. Watching 318 minutes of Karel Beran talking and Jason Walker asking questions, I noticed that this was by no means an ordinary conversation. Walker asked short questions and offered nothing in return. He never interrupted Mr Beran, but neither did he ever help him. If Mr Beran stopped and was clearly upset, Walker was silent and after a minute Mr Beran would continue. Once Walker asked Mr Beran what his Auschwitz number was. Mr Beran said he had forgotten and rolled up his sleeve to look but he

---

114 Notes accompanying Karel Beran's 1997 interview, *dornsife.usc.edu*, accessed 22 October 2012. (In 2006 the Survivors of the Shoah Visual History Foundation became part of the Dana and David Dornsife College of Letters, Arts and Sciences at the University of Southern California, and changed its name to become the University of Southern California Shoah Foundation Institute for Visual History and Education.)

couldn't see the number without his glasses. Mr Beran asked Walker to read it, but he didn't. He just asked a new question. I wondered if reading these numbers out loud and hearing them in his own voice would in some way make Walker feel as though he was one of the men who made the numbers.

I took from the overall style of the interview that there was a strict purpose to this conversation – to elicit and place on the record all Karel Beran could give of his personal experiences in the Holocaust – and that there would be no deviation from this purpose at any time.

*

During the interview Mr Beran often looks down and to the right in the space between a question and his answer. He says that there was always anti-Semitism in Austria where he lived as a young man, although it grew after Hitler took power. He speaks about two friends from the camps who stayed behind in Europe when he came to New Zealand. One, a social democrat activist, was imprisoned again after the war by the Soviet-led government of East Germany. Mr Beran shows photographs of this man's release years later. The other friend, Dr Glanz, he lost touch with during the long period after the war and before the collapse of the Soviet Union, when it was dangerous for people in Czechoslovakia to correspond with people in the West.

*

I learned that there was no impromptu decision to take ashes from Auschwitz. Karel Beran went back to Auschwitz with his friend Dr Armin Glanz in September 1946, to bring away some ashes to be interred in the Czech monument to the Unknown Soldier. Dr Glanz, whose name is on the caption in the Holocaust Gallery at the Auckland War Memorial Museum, was not, as I had imagined, an official of the Polish government of the time, with a possible Nazi past, but an official in the Czechoslovak government. Mr Beran and Dr Glanz had been together in Budy, a sub-camp of Auschwitz.

Mr Beran and Dr Glanz needed a special permit from the Russians and the Allied forces to enter Poland and it may have taken some time for this to be granted, but 'finally'[115] the men received a permit to enter Poland for one day. Perhaps this implied delay is the only reason for making the trip in September 1946.

The two men travelled, not in a train, which I had imagined as a mirror image of their deportation, but in a little Škoda sports car, which some friends with a farm had successfully hidden from both the Germans and the Russians, under straw and hay. There were, Mr Beran said, many happy times in this car, including his wedding trip with his wife.

---

115 Karel B., 'Interview by Survivors of the Shoah Visual History Foundation', 10 December 1997, Auckland, New Zealand, videotape 6.

Mr Beran said that the car was still at the farm. The son of the original owner had told Mr Beran that he would keep the car as long as he lived, as a memorial to Mr Beran. This was one of the most emotional moments in the interview. That Škoda sports car would be, as Mr Beran said a few seconds later in his practical voice, 'a very nice vintage car by now'.[116] At the end of the interview Mr Beran showed some photographs, one of which was of this car. I have the impression, from listening to Mr Beran's interview, that this little car is one of the most important objects in his life. I do not know what has happened to this very nice vintage car full of happy and sad memories since 1997.

On the day of the interview, in 1997, Mr Beran was not sure whether he and his friend went to Auschwitz on 10 or 16 September. Sometimes he has said one date and sometimes another, he says. The date could be checked by looking at his passport, he points out. I notice his concern that what he says should be accurate.

What follows is the story Mr Beran tells of his return to Auschwitz, as he tells it to Jason Walker on 10 December 1997.[117] Only comments pointing out topics of great emotion and a few joining words are mine.

Mr Beran and Dr Glanz crossed the border without much trouble and drove straight through the plains to Auschwitz.

---

116 Ibid.
117 Ibid., videotape 8.

In the main camp there were some maintenance people who had no objections to letting people have a look through. Already some documents had been gathered together like a camp museum. Apart from the memories that both of them were trying to cope with, there were no particular difficulties. The two men went on to Budy, where the local population had moved back into their houses. These houses had been occupied by the Waffen-SS during the war. At the Commander's house, which Mr Beran and Dr Glanz knew well, they saw a stork's nest on top of the chimney.

They remembered that for two or three years the stork family used to come back each summer, but now, in autumn 1946, the big nest was empty.

Most of the watchtowers and fences had been removed.

The two men spoke to the people there as best they could in Polish and Czech. The people were ordinary poor farmers who had been removed from the land by the Germans and were now back. They didn't know much about what was going on at Auschwitz, they said, which Mr Beran and Dr Glanz didn't want to believe. It was possible, Mr Beran added, if they were busy living, with very little time for anything else.[118]

The buildings were still there, including a blacksmith's shop which Mr Beran had helped to build. At Birkenau the

---

118 I note the lack of a final conclusion.

crematoria were partly demolished. There they gathered the ashes they had set out to collect.

The day ended with a lot of sad memories, back at a town on the Czech–Polish border. The men sat at their hotel, watching flames coming out of the huge chimneys of a local steelworks. At this point in the interview Mr Beran is weeping. Just like the crematorium, he says. Neither of the men could sleep, so they packed up at midnight and drove home.

That was it, Mr Beran says, trying to end this story.

Mr Beran kept a small part of the ashes and nobody knew about it. The rest went to Prague and were at some stage interred at the Tomb of the Unknown Warrior.

That ended the journey. He tries again.

The ashes I kept for fifty years here, he says, thinking some part may be my parents. As I grew older I thought they should be put to peace. With the help of the Jewish Community and Sol and Ruth Filler and the very active support of Rabbi Lawrence, the ashes were laid in a little sealed container at the foot of the Holocaust Memorial with a small stone notice telling the story that happened, on the 23rd of November 1997. Last month.

That's the end of the story. This is his last try. He succeeds. There are tears on his cheeks.

The interviewer says 'Thank you.'

*

Earlier, in tape 7, the interviewer had invited Mr Beran to give a message for the future. This is his message.

> The general message is like it was. There shouldn't be a war. The special message is that any racial discrimination should be avoided at all costs. I was always for this.

*

The wind blows

It is the Jewish custom to place a stone on a grave to help the dead to dissolve into dust and to show them that in that moment, someone remembers them, whether as air or sparks or dust. Every year, at the United Nations Holocaust Remembrance Day ceremony at the Makara cemetery, the survivors place a stone to show they were there. The wind blows. The pine trees bend. After that, anyone who wishes may place a stone. The stones do not make anything. They are just stones.

*

Acknowledgements

Lost and Gone Away began as a doctoral thesis at the International Institute of Modern Letters at Victoria University of Wellington. I would like to acknowledge the generous support of my PhD supervisors Bill Manhire and Chris Price and from my classmates in the IIML PhD programme: Pip Adam, Maxine Alterio, Michalia Arathimos, Dave Fleming, Tina Makereti, Lorry Patchett, Stephanie de Montalk, Laurence Fearnley, Hannah McKie, Gavin McGibbon and Steven Toussaint. Thanks also to Damien Wilkins, Katie Hardwick-Smith and Clare Moleta for assistance at key moments. It has been a privilege to be part of this writing community.

I am grateful for two specific sources of inspiration for 'Point Last Seen'. The use of categories to differentiate missing persons' circumstances is repeated in much of the literature on search and rescue techniques. I have used categories and some terminology from Robert J. Koester's *Lost Person Behavior*. Novelist Jordi Puntí stimulated my thoughts on the collective narrative, both in *Lost Luggage* and in conversations at the Writers Week in Wellington in 2014.

My debts and borrowings in 'The panorama machine' and 'I ring the bell anyway' will be obvious.

I received financial support from a Victoria Doctoral Scholarship, the Victoria University Faculty of Humanities and Social Sciences Research Fund, the Joe and Eve Major Trust and Creative New Zealand. Thanks to all involved.

Thanks to the Beran family, Kitty Hilton, Inge Woolf and Claire Bruell for their support with the project at critical points. Thanks also to Benjamin Geissler, Navina Clemerson, Avril Alba and John Leuthart for feedback during the project, to Alison Chetwin for her active support during my time at New Zealand Police and to Jeanette Schollum, Lynn Davidson and Hinemoana Baker for their company and sage words. Thanks to my mother Lesley Jenner for her consistent encouragement. And a special thanks to Ken Muir for some very significant ideas.

My greatest debt is to my partner Tony Pine who encouraged me to begin a PhD and has supported me and the project in every possible way. Arohanui, Tony.

Lynn Jenner